D1004029

THE GAMBLING TIMES GUIDE TO
HARNESS RACING

BY IGOR KUSYSHYN, Ph.D.,
AL STANLEY AND SAM DRAGICH

A GAMBLING TIMES BOOK

DISTRIBUTED BY
LYLE STUART
Secaucus, N.J.

**THE GAMBLING TIMES GUIDE
TO HARNESS RACING**
Copyright © 1984 Gambling Times Incorporated

ISBN: 0-89746-002-2

Distributed by Lyle Stuart, Inc.

Manufactured in the United States of America
Printed and Bound by Kingsport Press
First Printing—January 1984

Editor: *Linda Lee Talbert*
Cover by Jerome D. Holder

All material presented in this book is offered as information to the
reader. No inducement to gamble is intended or implied.

Other *Gambling Times* Books
Available—Current Releases

(See page 134 for details)

Poker Books

According to Doyle
by Doyle Brunson
Caro On Gambling by Mike Caro
Caro's Book of Tells by Mike Caro
The GT Official Rules of Poker
by Mike Caro
Poker For Women by Mike Caro
Poker Without Cards by Mike Caro
Win, Places and Pros
by Tex Sheahan

Blackjack Books

**The Beginner's Guide to Winning
Blackjack** by Stanley Roberts
The GT Guide to Blackjack
by Stanley Roberts and others
Million Dollar Blackjack
by Ken Uston

Casino Games

The GT Guide to Casino Games
by Len Miller
The GT Guide to Craps
by N.B. Winkless, Jr.

General Interest Books

**According to GT: The Rules of
Gambling Games**
by Stanley Roberts

**The GT Guide to Gaming Around
the World**
**The GT Guide to Systems That
Win, Volumes I and II**
**The GT Guide to Winning
Systems, Volumes I and II**
**GT Presents Winning Systems and
Methods, Volumes I and II**
The Mathematics of Gambling
by Dr. Edward O. Thorp
Odds: Quick and Simple
by Mike Caro
P$yching Out Vegas
by Marvin Karlins, Ph.D.
Winning By Computer
by Dr. Donald Sullivan

Sports Betting Books

**The GT Guide to Basketball
Handicapping** by Barbara Nathan
**The GT Guide to Football
Handicapping** by Bob McCune
**The GT Guide to Greyhound
Racing** by William E. McBride
The GT Guide to Jai Alai
by William R. Keevers
**The GT Guide to Thoroughbred
Racing** by R.G. Denis

The following *Gambling Times* books are scheduled for release in September 1984:

Poker Books

Caro's Poker Encyclopedia
by Mike Caro

Free Money: How to Win in the Cardrooms of California
by Michael Wiesenberg

New Poker Games
by Mike Caro

PROfile: The World's Greatest Poker Players
by Stuart Jacobs

The Railbird by Rex Jones

Tales Out of Tulsa
by Bobby Baldwin

World Class Poker, Play by Play by Mike Caro

General Interest Books

Caro On Computer Gambling
by Mike Caro

The Casinos of the Caribbean
by Stanley Roberts

The Casino Gourmet: Great Recipes from the Master Chefs of Las Vegas
by Stanley Roberts

The Casino Gourmet: Great Recipes from the Master Chefs of Atlantic City
by Stanley Roberts

The Casino Gourmet: Great Recipes from the Master Chefs of Reno/Lake Tahoe
by Stanley Roberts

The Casino Gourmet: Great Recipes from the Master Chefs of the Caribbean
by Stanley Roberts

The Casino Gourmet: Great Recipes from the Master Chefs of Europe
by Stanley Roberts

The Casino Gourmet: Great Recipes from the Master Chefs of the Orient
by Stanley Roberts

A Gambler's View of History
by Mike Caro

Gambling Greats: Profiles of the World's Greatest Gamblers by Pamela Shandel

The GT Quiz Book
by Mike Caro

How the Superstars Gamble
by Ron Delpit

How to Win at Gaming Tournaments by Haven Earle Haley

You're Comped: How to Be a Casino Guest by Len Miller

Sports Betting Books

Cramer on Harness Race Handicapping
by Mark Cramer

Cramer on Thoroughbred Handicapping
by Mark Cramer

TABLE OF CONTENTS

ACKNOWLEDGEMENTS

We are very pleased with this primer on harness racing. It took the cooperation of many devotees of the sport to put it together, and we know the primer will add to your enjoyment of the sport.   In this space we gratefully acknowledge the assistance of the people at the racetracks and organizations who took the time to speak and correspond with us.

We would like to thank, in particular, the officials of the United States Trotting Association (U.S.T.A.), the Canadian Trotting Association (C.T.A.), the Ontario Jockey Club (O.J.C.), and Windsor Raceway.

Our thanks also to Glen Girard for the cartoon illustrations, to Tony Piccinato for the photographs, and to Gail Morris for the typing.

PREFACE

Welcome to the wonderful world of harness racing.

Gambling Times is pleased to have these distinguished professional handicappers combine their talents to produce a primer about the exciting standardbred sport in *The Gambling Times Guide To Harness Racing*. This book has been written in the same honest, sensitive and perceptive style that has characterized their former works.

Canada is known throughout the industry as home base for many of harness racing's great drivers, trainers and breeders. Canada is the home of many world harness champions. These Canadian harness authors and handicappers are no exception. Their fresh, lucid commentary carefully and thoroughly examines every corner of the harness track. They illuminate the backstretch, advise on etiquette at the track, present advantages of horse ownership, explain the roles and rules by which participants in the sulky sport play, describe how to watch the races, how to wager, and much more.

It's all here in *The Gambling Times Guide To Harness Racing*. All the information that is necessary to understand fully the entire harness racing scene is contained in this book. Whether you are a racetrack novice or a regular, if you have been seduced by the trotting and pacing scene, then this book is for you. We at *Gambling Times* are proud to add it to our collection of outstanding gaming literature. Again, we are pleased to welcome you with this primer to the wonderful world of harness racing. Good luck!

Stanley R. Sludikoff, Publisher

PART ONE
The "How To" World of Harness Racing

Chapter 1

A Brief History of the Sport

While harness racing is generally considered to be a native American sport, traces of it can be found some 3,000 years back in history. And its roots, like those of most American citizens, can be found in other lands and in other breeds.

The modern version of American harness racing is generally conceded to have commenced in 1806, when records of sorts began to be kept and a gelding by the name of *Yankee* trotted a mile in less than three minutes for the first time.

The standardbred breed — both trotters and pacers are called standardbreds — received its most important transfusion in 1788. In that year, a grey thoroughbred called *Messenger* arrived in America from England to become the patriarch of a family of fine trotting horses. An infusion of Morgan horse blood served to enrich the breed.

The harness sport received another massive shot in the arm with the birth of *Hambletonian*, a descendant of *Messenger*, in 1849. *Hambletonian*, owned by William Rysdyk of Chester, New York, raced only sparingly, but quickly proved himself to be history's greatest progenitor of gait and speed. All but a very few of today's trotters and pacers trace back to *Hambletonian*, and it's small wonder that the most famous harness race of them all bears his name.

Harness racing's popularity has soared and sizzled, faded and fizzled over its long American history. It was immensely popular in the 1800's, but fell from favor when the automobile arrived on the scene to dislodge the horse as a means of transportation.

The return to popularity in the 1940's stemmed from several factors. New York State approved pari-mutuel betting on the races, a group of intrepid investors proved that nighttime harness racing could succeed by offering races under the lights at Roosevelt Raceway on Long Island, and a man named Stephen G. Phillips developed the mobile starting gate.

Through both the thick and the thin, great horses arrived on the scene to save the sport from extinction and to give it a healthy push as it bounced back to popularity. *Flora Temple,* the "bobtail nag" of Stephen Foster's Camptown Races, was an immense favorite of the 1850's, *Goldsmith Maid* won 350 races in the 1870's, and *Dan Patch,* a pacer, was a sort of national institution shortly after the turn of the century, drawing crowds of 60,000 or more and having tobacco, toys, washing machines and dance steps named after him.

Pacing horses wormed their way into harness racing hearts in the 1860's, earning their right to compete over the strenuous objections of many purists. If pacing supporters had not persisted, the sport, the nation, and the world would never have heard of such modern heroes as *Bret Hanover, Albatross* and *Niatross.* A little over a century later, four out of five harness horses now racing are pacers, and many persons in the sport are concerned about preserving the trotting gait.

Harness racing in the 1980's is still a healthy, vibrant sport, despite the relatively recent birth and growth of off-track betting, teletracks that offer wagering on races in theatres, and the spread of casino gambling. Nearly 30 million persons attend the races each year, sampling the sport at some 60 pari-mutuel tracks or at more than 400 fairs.

The harness sport is extremely popular in Canada, Australia, New Zealand, and in most of the nations of Europe, although only trotters are raced in the vast majority of the European nations.

Harness racing is a burgeoning factor in the economies of many states across the nation. Tax revenues and jobs have resulted wherever pari-mutuel harness tracks have sprouted, with states, counties and cities sharing in the bonanza. The growth of standardbred breeding — several states have rich racing programs to stimulate it — has been obvious in recent years, adding whole new industries to the economies of some states.

More than 12,000 men and women are now driving harness horses in races across the land, some of them amateurs, some of them professionals. Nearly 50,000 persons hold membership in the U.S. Trotting Association, which keeps the sport's records and helps to govern it. Tens of thousands more are indirectly involved in the sport.

The various "homes" of harness racing range from the smallest country fair, where only an afternoon or two of racing is offered each year, to the handsome and huge Meadowlands Sports Complex at East Rutherford, New Jersey. Some 18,000 fans, betting some $125 each, attend The Meadowlands each night it offers harness racing.

Standardbred yearlings have sold for as much as $300,000, while drivers like Herve Filion and Bill Haughton each have already driven horses to more than $30 million in earnings during their careers.

Harness racing is big business. And it's here to stay.

In A Class By Himself

Chapter 2

How to Plan a Night at the Races

What to Wear

Raceway officials wish your visit to their plant to be as enjoyable and comfortable as possible. Therefore, what one wears to the track should reflect his own particular taste and comfort. But one's clothing should not be offensive to others either in the grandstand or the clubhouse. While almost anything goes (as long as it is in good taste) in the grandstand a dress code is often enforced in the clubhouse. Most clubhouse dress codes prohibit jeans, cutoffs, and T-shirts on men, and some insist on jackets in the clubhouse dining room.

One is never overdressed in the clubhouse. Since all are heated in the winter and most are air-conditioned in the summer, one should dress for the occasion. Ties, sweaters, turtlenecks and open-necked shirts are appropriate for men; while dresses, pantsuits, gowns and skirts are suitable for women. If you are at all concerned with being turned back at the clubhouse, then a simple phone call to the raceway management should answer your questions concerning proper attire.

What to Bring

Almost everyone who visits the racetrack does so to be entertained. If you do not wish to miss out on any of the action, both on the track and at trackside, then you should bring binoculars. Good binoculars measure 10×50 with extra wide field and low glare lens. These are especially effective at night. The wide angle permits you normally to hold the entire string of horses and sulkies in your vision without shifting your glasses.

At raceways where matinee racing is held, a pair of sunglasses will provide additional comfort. Other equipment for both the novice and the track regular could include: pencils, pens, a clipboard, and perhaps a stopwatch (for the more serious). And finally, don't forget to bring some money.

How Much Money To Bring

Major credit cards are acceptable to pay the tab in raceway dining rooms but are normally unacceptable for wagering at the mutuel windows. The smallest amount that any patron can wager at any one time is $2.00. Therefore, if you wish to wager in all races of a typical 10-race program, then you should set aside a minimum of $20.00. An evening at the races is not inexpensive. Depending on your personal eating and seating preferences, be prepared to pay for parking, grandstand or clubhouse admission, a past performance program, snacks or meals, preferred seating, drinks, and a tip sheet which advises which horses to bet.

Having A Race Named After Your Group

How would you like to have a race named after you in honor of your birthday, anniversary, group or special event? Then, to top it off, how would you like to have your picture taken in the winner's circle afterwards?

Most raceways in North America are able to provide such services in one form or another. Raceway managements are continually striving to make your visit to their plant entertaining, memorable, and enjoyable. To ensure that *perfect* night, planning ahead is important.

If yours is a small party, telephone the raceway's clubhouse dining room and make a reservation through the Maitre'D. This should be done well in advance—two or more weeks before for best results. And do ask for a table on the "glass" (at the windows) or on a tier near the finish line. For larger groups these arrangements can be made through the *Groups Reservation Desk*. In the event your raceway does not have a dining room, a call to the public relations director will normally provide the necessary service.

Should you be at the racetrack a day or two before your party, check out the details again with the Maitre'D. A tip to him then or on reservation night is quite appropriate since you do not want to be disappointed. If you are unable to check ahead in person a telephone call will suffice. In any case, the Maitre'D will remind you to arrive early, an hour or more before post time. He wants to assure you of getting a good table and ample time to dine before the first race begins.

Fortunately, raceway dining rooms across North America have developed fine reputations for good food at reasonable prices. So the rest is up to you and the capabilities of the raceway's public relations department. And don't be surprised if you see the *occasion* flashed on the tote board or your name announced over the public address system when you arrive at the winner's circle for your photo!

GETTING EVEN FOR THE NIGHT

Chapter 3

How to Read a Program

If you have been to the runners (thoroughbred racing) you are probably familiar with the popularity of the *Daily Racing Form* at the track. No such comparable "bible" is available in harness racing, nor is one necessary. Every harness track in North America is equipped to process and print all of the up-to-date information about a horse's past performances in an official program. This is made possible through a computer link-up with the major governing bodies of harness racing in both countries, namely: the United States Trotting Association (U.S.T.A.) and the Canadian Trotting Association (C.T.A.). Their service is open 24 hours per day. It is invaluable to any racing secretary's office as horses move from track to track across this continent. In fact, this service is so sophisticated and current that, often, the racing secretary's office has all the information it really needs before a new horse enters the stable area from another raceway.

The raceway's official past performance program is the scorecard one needs to interpret and understand the evening's events. Programs are generally available for purchase just inside the gates at any raceway. If you wish to preview and study the card beforehand, these programs usually can be bought at newsstands and other commercial outlets in the raceway's area. Although one can purchase a program for the next night's racing card at the track late in the evening, the public not in attendance customarily must wait until morning to buy it on the streets.

Every raceway prints a table and diagram to help the track patron better interpret the abbreviations and symbols used in a particular program. But, quite often, this information alone is not of sufficient use for the novice to the sport. The data which follows should be of some educational benefit in reading any program.

About the Race: Primarily, the top of any program page lists the race identification data from the racing secretary's office: the race number, the purse, the distance, the condition (claiming, type of condition, etc.), and even the saddle cloth color. Saddle cloth colors and numbers aid in identifying specific horses as they are warming up on the track between races. All the horses entered in the same race will wear similar saddle cloth colors. To save you time from searching through the program for saddle cloth colors information, raceways usually print a color code on the rail near the tote board. Locate this for yourself the next time you visit the track.

About Past Perfomances: This concise box of statistics contains just about all the information one needs to handicap a race. The past performance racing lines are most important. They are printed in chronological order with the most recent race appearing at the top, then the horse's next-to-last race recorded next, and so on. Often six or more past performance lines are shown. Each usually shows the date of the race, temperature, condition, amount of purse, leader's time at the 1st, 2nd, 3rd quarter, winner's time, position of this horse at each of the calls, this horse's final time closing odds to $1.00, this horse's driver, and the win, place and show horses.

Also contained in this box are: Life Time Statistics (the horse's lifetime mark for the mile, the size of track and his age when the record was set, and his lifetime earnings as of last December 31); Driver/Trainer Information (listing tonight's colors and the name of the trainer); Owner Breeding Data (color, sex of horse as well as the names of the horse's sire, dam, and dam's sire); and Current Records (showing a number of starts and in-the-money finishes for current year and year prior, earnings this year and last, and best winning times for both years).

Figure 3-1 shows the kind of information one can expect to find in any raceway program exploring the abbreviated statistics used when compiling past performances.

About the Morning Line: The track official responsible for setting the opening odds must adhere to certain rules as determined by the governing bodies in harness racing. In reality, this official, the track handicapper, attempts to give the true odds as he sees them. Based on his calculations, these odds represent each horse's chances of winning that particular race. The track patrons, however, do not always agree with the track handicapper. When the public overrates or underrates certain horses the effect gives rise to a gambling concept known as an *overlay* or *underlay*. Check these important concepts in the *Glossary of Terms* contained in this book. The morning line odds normally appear with each horse's post position number.

The *trackman's selections* traditionally appear somewhere on the page of each race. These numbers represent his predictions for the final outcome of the race. If his selections are 3-9-4, this means that he predicts that #3 will *win*, #9 will *place*, and #4 will *show*.

About Racing Results Charts: The results chart for a particular race is generally printed in the program two days after the race is completed. Racing lines for each horse are shown charting each horse's position at all the calls from start to finish. Those track patrons who become serious handicappers find the charts useful in future handicapping. They look for *keys* they may have missed in observing the race two days before in hopes of gaining an edge on the public. Included in the results charts is the following: quarter times for the leader, each horse's finish time and closing odds at post time, the public favorite, the mutuel payoffs, and the names of the horsemen who made any claim in the race.

Figure 3-2 shows a typical Results Chart.

About the Tip Sheet: The average track patron likes to get assistance for his handicapping. Public handicappers today publish their selections in the newspapers, announce them over the air (on radio and TV), and some even tout them on tip sheets on the track's premises. Tip sheets can be purchased at the track and provide the harness fan with another opinion about the outcome of each race. Track tipsters give the raceway a percentage return on their sales for the privilege of selling the tip sheet at the track. Some racetracks hire a public handicapper to write the tip sheet each night and often will pay him a bonus whenever his predictions are substantially accurate.

Figure 3-1: How To Read The Program

The horse's head number, saddle cloth number, program number, mutuel number and post position are the same except where there is an entry in the race. The initials following the horse's name represent color and sex, figures denote age. The names following are the horse's sire, dam and sire of dam in that order. Under the horse's name are his lifetime earnings and lifetime record preceded by his age when record was made up to January 1 of the current year. Following the lifetime earnings is the name of the driver, his date of birth, weight and his colors. Next is the horse's best winning time on a half-mile, five-eighths, three-quarter or mile track for last year and the current racing season, followed by his starts and the number of wins, seconds, thirds in purse races and his money winnings. Beneath the horse's name are records of his six most recent races. They read from bottom to top, therefore the top line is the horse's last race.

The date of the race is followed by the name of the track. All tracks are half-mile unless followed by the figure (1) which means that it is a mile track or ($\frac{3}{4}$) which is a three-quarter mile track, etc. Then is noted the Purse, condition of the track on the day of the race, the Conditions of the race or if a Claiming Race the Claiming Price. Race distance, time of leading horse at the $\frac{1}{4}$, $\frac{1}{2}$ and $\frac{3}{4}$, follow, then comes the winner's time. The figures that follow in order show the post position of the horse, his position at the $\frac{1}{4}$, $\frac{1}{2}$, $\frac{3}{4}$, stretch with lengths behind except for the leading horse whose number denotes lengths ahead, and finish with beaten lengths. If he was a winner, it shows how far ahead of the second horse and the losers show how far they were behind the winning horse. The next figure shows the horse's actual time in that race. Whenever a small "°" appears after the calls, it denotes that the horse raced on the outside at least one-quarter of a mile. In some instances these figures won't appear because the track at which the horse raced did not have its races charted. Then follows the closing odds to the dollar, the horse's driver, and the order of finish, giving the names of the first three horses, temperature and time allowance due to cold weather.

KEY TO ABBREVIATIONS

Horses' Colors	Horses' Sex	Track Conditions	Finish Information	Wagering Information	Race Classes
b—bay	c—colt	ft—fast	P—Placing	N.B.—No Betting	Cd—Condition Race
blk—black	f—filly	gd—good	ns—nose	N.R.—Not Reported	10000 clm—Claiming price
br—brown	g—gelding	sy—sloppy	hd—head	°—favorite	Ec—Early closing event
ch—chestnut	h—horse	sl—slow	nk—neck	e—entry	FA—free for all
gr—gray	m—mare	my—muddy	dh—dead heat	f—field	JFA—Junior Free for all
ro—roan	ri—ridgling	hy—heavy	dis—distanced over 25		Hcp—Handicap Race
			lengths behind winner		Inv—Invitational Race

Racing Information

°—Raced on outside for at least $\frac{1}{4}$ mile
°°—Raced three wide
x—horse broke at this point
i—races without hopples
ix—break caused by interference
i—horse interfered with at this point
Qua (dr)—Qualifying Race for Driver
Qua (h–d)—Qualifying Race for both horse and driver
T.Dis—Time for race was disallowed on this horse because of a placing due to other than a lapped on break at finish.
(J)—Horse registered with New Jersey Breeders Association.
St.—Stable in which horse is trained

B.E.—broken equipment
ax—break caused by accident
acc—accident
ex—equipment break
dnf—did not finish
BAR—Barred in wagering
H.N.—head number

(1)—Mile Track
($\frac{3}{4}$)—$\frac{3}{4}$ Track
($\frac{1}{2}$)—$\frac{1}{2}$ Track
z—horse claimed
(c)—Conventional Sulky

Lc—Late Closing Event
Mdn—Maiden
Mat—Matinee (no purse)
nw—Non-Winners
nw300ps—Average Earnings was less than $300 per start
Opn—Open To All
Opt Clm—Optional Claiming
Pref—Preferred
Qua—Qualifying Race
Stk—Stake Race
T—Time Trial
w—Winners - over
F–M—Fillies & Mares
NJSS—New Jersey Sires Stake

PROGRAM and HEAD NUMBER	Date of Race	Track Raced On Distance of Race Sulky Type of Purse	Track Condition Type of Race	Condition or Claiming Price	Time at $\frac{1}{4}$	Time at $\frac{1}{2}$	Time at $\frac{3}{4}$	Time of Winner	Post Position at $\frac{1}{4}$	Position at $\frac{1}{2}$	Position at $\frac{3}{4}$	Stretch Position and Lengths	Finish Position and Lengths Behind Winner	Horse's Actual Time	Equivalent odds to 1.00	Driver	Best Win Time of Year	Name of Winner	Name of Second Horse	Name of Third Horse	Temperature and Time Allowance

4 SENOR SKIPPER br h, 4, by Meadow Skipper—Senorita Cheetah by Adios Paul   Trainer-E. Spruce
Ernie & Marion Spruce, Rexdale, Ont.   M(1)1:53³ 1978 29 10 4 5 266,010

7-22 M¹⊗ 25000 ft Opn mi 27² :55³1:23⁴1:53³ 3 4 3° 1 1⁶ 1¹⁴ 1:53³ *1.50(B.Webster)SnrSkppr,KrryGld,ShdysdTrx 89–0

14

Figure 3-2: Results Chart

GREENWOOD RACEWAY **MONDAY, JUNE 8, 1981**

ATT. 8,356 HNDL $1,189,186 WEATHER cloudy TEMP. 16°C TRACK Sloppy

Horse	PP	¼	½	¾	Str.	Fin.	Time	SpdRt	Driver	Odds	Comments
RACE 1 (7:31)	**PACE**				**CONDITIONED**						**PURSE $2,600**
Mamart Bold Ann	7	6	7°¾	6^{4}	6^{4}¼	1¾	2:05^{1}	70	WapK	42.30	charged outside
Best Of Wall	6	7	6^{6}¾	4^{o2}¾	$4x^{2}$	2¾	2:05^{2}	69	WalD	2.70	big effort
Captain Outrageous	4	1	3^{1}¼	5^{2}¾	5^{2}¾	3^{1}¾	2:05^{3}	68	StrT	◆1.30	shuffled, fought
Alba Rose	1	4	4^{2}¼	2^{o1}	2^{1}	4^{2}	2:05^{3}	68	WalL	3.45	outpaced to wire
Logan Star	3	5	5^{5}¼	7^{5}½	7^{5}¾	5^{2}	2:05^{3}	68	GilF	24.05	steady effort
Hornby Steve	5	2°	1hd	$3b^{1}$¼	3^{2}	6^{2}¼	2:05^{3}	68	CokW	6.65	late room on rail
Maedir	2	3	2°hd	1^{1}	1^{1}	7^{2}¼	2:05^{3}	68	WapR	10.00	weakened late
(7) 86.60/25.00/11.30 (6) 5.00/3.60 (4) 3.30											:29^{4}1:01^{4}1:32 2:05^{1}TV 6
RACE 2 (7:52)	**TROT**				**FREE FOR ALL HANDICAP**						**PURSE $13,000**
Arnie's Suwannee	4	2	2^{1}½	2^{1}¼	2¾	1^{1}¼	2:04^{3}	73	DavB	2.90	sat perfectly
Horton's Miss	6	1°	1^{1}½	1^{1}¼	1¾	2^{1}¼	2:04^{4}	72	CokW	◆.85	used taking lead
Honest Rico	3	4	4^{4}¾	4^{3}¾	$3x^{2}$	$x3^{2}$½	†2:05	71 †pl5	SteH	8.80	untimely break
Spring Flight	2	3	3^{3}	3^{2}½	5^{4}¾	4^{2}¾	†2:05^{1}	70 †pl3	MacN	11.15	tired late
Keystone Kathy	5	5	5^{6}¼	5^{o5}¼	$4x^{3}$½	$x5^{3}$	†2:05^{1}	70 †pl6	WapR	5.45	outside rush
Jumbo Jet	x1	6	6^{7}½	6^{5}½	6^{5}½	6^{5}	†2:05^{3}	68 †pl4	WalD	12.20	a present
(4) 7.80/3.50/4.00 (6) 2.40/2.70 (2) 4.20											
DAILY DOUBLE (7-4) $399.90 QUINELLA (4-6) $7.90											:29^{4}1:01^{4}1:33^{2}2:04^{3}TV 6
RACE 3 (8:19)	**PACE**				**CONDITIONED**						**PURSE $2,600**
Kalila Katie	4	2	3^{2}½	2^{o1}½	2^{1}	1ns	2:05^{1}	70	CokW	4.25	positioned well
Barney Hanover	1	4	1^{1}¼	1^{1}½	1^{1}	2ns	2:05^{1}	70	CorM	7.85	tough foe
Dark Alert	5	1	2^{1}¼	3^{1}½	3^{2}½	3^{2}½	2:05^{3}	68	WapK	12.45	early threat
Diamond Girl	9	6	6^{6}	7^{5}	6^{5}¾	4^{3}¾	2:06	64	ConS	2.40	late room between
Tom	3	3	4^{4}	$4b^{3}$	4^{3}¾	5^{4}	2:06	66	WalL	◆2.00	
Countess Dana	7	9	9^{8}½	9^{7}¼	8^{8}½	6^{4}	2:06	66	DufJ	15.85	rolling late
Turn To Soozie	6	8	8^{7}¼	8^{6}¼	9^{9}	7^{4}½	2:06	66	WilJ	12.20	
Highland Justice	2	7	7^{6}	6^{o4}¾	7^{7}½	8^{7}	2:06^{3}	63	StrT	28.70	
Brinston Bret	8	5	5^{5}	5^{o3}	5^{5}¼	9^{15}	2:08^{1}	55	WapR	25.10	weakened in lane
(4) 10.50/4.80/4.30 (1) 7.70/7.00 (5) 6.70 EXACTOR (4-1) $111.20											:30^{2}1:03^{3}1:34^{1}2:05^{1}TV 6
RACE 4 (8:42)	**TROT**				**OAKVILLE STAKES**						**PURSE $26,300**
Sparkle Hanover	3	4	4^{o2}¾	2°ns	1^{1}½	1hd	2:07^{2}	59	WalL	9.00e	big effort
Armbro Whirl	9	6	6^{6}¼	5^{2}¾	5^{4}	2hd	2:07^{2}	59	GarG	◆1.30	late charge betw'n
Dream Of Fame	4	9	9^{12}	7^{5}½	6^{5}½	3^{1}¼	2:07^{3}	58	EaiL	16.60	big late gains
Royal Future	5	1°	2^{1}½	3^{1}¼	3^{2}¾	4^{5}	2:08^{2}	54	WapR	2.00	pushed early
Unexpected Speed	8	3°	1^{1}½	1ns	2^{1}½	5^{7}	2:08^{4}	52	CleB	9.00e	weakened in lane
Armbro Waltz	2	5	5^{4}½	4^{o1}¼	4^{4}	6^{10}	2:09^{2}	49	SteH	39.25	
Naughty Miss	7	8	7^{7}¾	6^{4}¼	$7x^{7}$	7^{13}	2:10	46	RitT	37.30	
Island Lore	10	10	$ix10^{13}$	10^{24}	10^{21}	8^{17}	2:10^{4}	42	WalD	5.15	road trouble
Pegway's Princess	6	7°	8^{9}	8^{12}	8^{15}	9^{17}	2:10^{4}	42	KirP	109.20	
Whirlaway Wendy	11	x11	11^{23}	9^{18}	9^{20}	10^{18}	2:11	41	LeaH	97.95	
Elwadar Sue	1	2	3^{2}¾	$x11^{31}$	11^{37}	11dis			CroG	16.65	away fast, broke
(1) 20.00/6.00/4.60 (8) 3.50/3.20 (4) 6.40											:30^{1}1:02 1:34 2:07^{2}TV 6

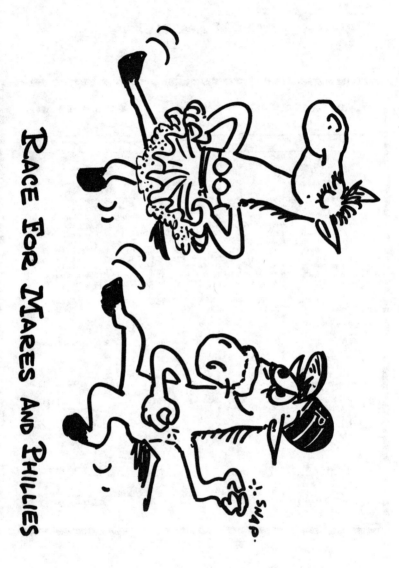

RACE FOR MARES AND PHILLIES

Chapter 4

How to Watch a Race

Unlike the thoroughbreds (the runners), harness racehorses today almost always pace or trot in races of one mile. Hence, the term *standardbred,* as they all conform to the *mile standard* at one gait (trot or pace). The race itself is an exciting event to behold, pitting not only driving strategies and abilities against each other but also the racing condition and hearts of the horses as well. From start to finish, on the straightaways (stretches) and on the curves (turns), several things can happen in a harness race. For example, horses can *break stride, get boxed in, lock wheels,* or *get parked out.* Each of these and other occurences during a harness race affect the outcome (finish positions) of all the horses.

Let us now examine all of the factors which make a harness race exciting to gain a better understanding of horse, man, and machine.

Standardbreds Separated by Speed and Style

The majority of standardbred race winners can cover the mile distance today at a speed from 1:57 to 2:07. Anyone who has been out to the harness races knows that these winning times were not achieved through an all-out spirit. In fact, the win may have resulted from one or more *moves* that the driver asked his horse to make during the race. A move, also known as a *brush,* can be defined as a *short burst of speed usually for about 1/16 of a mile.*

Some horsemen classify harness horses from best to worst on the basis of the number of moves a horse can make in a race. And this labeling has merit. For instance, a horse that is capable of making only one move during a race (often at the start or end) can be found among the cheaper claimers at the track ($5000 claiming or less). While a horse that can make two moves (usually one to get into position and the other for the final brush) is normally found in the mid-range claiming classes ($8000—$15,000) and some of the lower priced conditioned races. Now, horses that are able to exert high expenditures of energy three times during a race must be counted among the best at any racetrack. Such animals cutomarily show early speed at the start, stay in contention in the middle of the race, and then still have something in reserve for an explosive finish to the wire.

Most of the fans at a harness track, however, refer to harness horses by their racing style. Two of the most common are *front-runners* and *closers*. The front-runner races best when he's *on top* and able to control the pace of the race; if the horse is challenged for the lead he will try to fight it off and then hang on to win the race. The closer, on the other hand, lays back in good position gradually increasing his speed in the second half for a final all-out dash to the finish wire; these horses waste as little energy as possible in the first half and usually can be seen *parked out with cover* (behind another horse on the outside) intent on gaining on the leader.

What to Look for at the Start:

As the starting gate swings open some of the horses can be seen *leaving* (bursting to the front) while others will just settle in along the rail in single file and follow the leaders. Horses that leave are not necessarily front-runners. Some drivers will steer their horse in behind the leader *sitting in the golden chair*. They are hoping to be *pulled along in the vacuum* created by the leader, then when the leader begins to tire they will pull out and pass him.

On occasion, one or two horses will remain parked out just after the start because they cannot find a *hole* on the rail. Since these horses have already committed themselves (by showing early speed), they will usually continue moving ahead until they take the lead. Often it costs these horses the win at the end of the race because they travel a much faster first quarter and a half than they intended. Such horses will try to slow the pace of the race down a bit once they've gained the lead to give them time to catch a second wind.

Then, again, some horses are *pullers*. They race to the front and attempt to go at full speed the entire race. If you observe carefully you can see these horses almost *pulling the hands and arms off* their drivers as they attempt to harness this energy. Pullers tend to lead the pack until about the final 1/8th or 1/16th, and then appear nearly to stop from fatigue allowing other horses to pass them.

Perhaps the most distressing sight at the start of a race, outside of an accident, is having a horse break stride. There are always a few horses at a track which have difficulty going to the gate — they seem afraid of it and lose their concentration. Others break because of interference, broken equipment, or simply from trying to move at a faster, uncontrollable pace. In any case, a horse which breaks stride must conform to certain legislated rules of harness racing. The driver of a horse which breaks must move his horse to the outside as soon as it is clear, and must lose ground until he gets his horse back on stride.

What to Watch for in Mid-Race:

Once the horses have settled in behind the leader they often will remain that way until just before the half-mile pole unless the lead horse slows the pace down considerably. If this happens, one of the nearest following horses will pull out and try to take the lead. It should be noted here that drivers who slow down the pace an excessive amount are subject to a fine by the judges.

As the horses near the half-mile pole, two tiers of horses begin to appear. The horses parked on the outside usually represent the closers who are attempting gradually to improve their position. These parked out horses are in the best position to overtake the leader towards the finish. All horses that tire veer away from the rail enabling those behind to slip by them on the inside.

When the horses reach the final 1/8th pole they begin to *fan out* for their final brush. Horses behind this wall of horseflesh can be viewed darting in and out looking for a hole to explode through. Occasionally, a horse will experience a *speed break* just before or at the finish wire. This could change the outcome of the race. Horses that break *under* the wire do not have their official finish position altered. However, if a horse breaks before the wire and is overlapped by another horse or horses, a situation arises known as a *lapped on break*. Here the horse which broke is set down a position or two.

POST PARADE

20

Chapter 5

How to Read the Tote Board

The large tote boards which grace the infields of harness tracks across North America provide the track patron with a wealth of information. Modern computerized tote boards instantly flash such information as current odds, gimmick payoffs, driver changes, and money bet in the Win, Place, and Show Pools. At first, the newcomer may be overwhelmed by the constant updating of all the figures on the board. But, once he understands what is involved, reading the tote board becomes easier with successive trips to his favorite raceway.

Public relations personnel at racetracks are aware of their duty to educate their fans. So, from time to time, they will publish an easy-to-read illustration of "How to Read the Tote Board" in their printed programs. This is a must for the beginner. If your track doesn't provide this service, just give them a call.

How the Tote Functions

The *Pari-mutuel* wagering system is one wherein the public wagers among themselves. The public does not wager against the track, rather the raceway holds and administers the "pot" of total monies wagered on every race. For this service the track retains 17-18% of the mutuel *handle* (all the monies wagered on a particular card). From the *track take*, the sponsoring government agency, the track itself, and the horsemen (in purses) get their shares. The remaining 82-83% is distributed proportionately as payoffs to those patrons holding winning tickets.

The bettor never bets against the track — only against other bettors. Thus, it is the public money only which is displayed in accumulating figures on the board. Whereas, formerly, information flow was slow when it was done by hand and open to error, today most totes are computerized giving absolute odds and correct payoffs. This fully automatic system has speeded up the wagering process and undoubtedly has made a visit to the track more enjoyable, and less frustrating, for track patrons and raceway personnel alike.

Every wager is automatically totalled on the board when the ticket is punched out of the mutuel machine. As the bets accumulate, the current odds are flashed to the public; then, when the race starts, a bell instantaneously sounds signalling the end of betting on that race. Each machine is electronically locked preventing anyone from betting after the race is started. A few moments later, the tote will flash the final odds and the totals wagered on each of the horses in all the pools. The first set of odds posted on the tote board when the mutuel windows open for a race is the *morning line*. The morning line is the track handicapper's estimate of each horse's chances of becoming the race winner. Then, when the race is declared *official* by the judges, the payoffs for each winning $2.00 Win, Place, and Show ticket will be displayed on the tote board.

Modern tote boards are capable of communicating even more information to track fans. Not only can important messages, advertisements, and handicapping data be displayed, but approximate *feature* payoff can be recorded as well. The alert handicapper sometimes spots patterns in the wagering here which helps him determine whether or not a horse is *live* (ready to exert a winning effort) tonight. The average fan, on the other hand, appreciates knowing the approximate payoff on his feature ticket. Features are also known as *gimmick* races (daily double, exacta, trifecta, quinella, etc.).

Figure 5-1 illustrates how to read a tote board.

Wait Till the Race is Declared Official

While the tote board is designed to give automatic results sometimes there is a delay in declaring a race official. The judges are responsible for causing this delay--perhaps they noticed *interference* during the race, a *break* before the start, a *lapped on break* at the finish, or even a *photo finish*. All of these factors have an effect upon the final result, so the judges trigger the *inquiry* sign. This simply means that they wish to review the *video replay* and either uphold or deny the objection.

If there is an infraction identified in any of the cases discussed in the preceding paragraphs, then the judges will *adjust* the final order of finish accordingly. Depending upon where the infraction took place and what effect it had on the other horses, the judges may *set back* the horse (and driver) one or more post positions. This action will be disappointing to fans holding "winning"tickets on the guilty horses, but it is costly to horsemen as well. When a horse is set back, the horsemen's share of the purse money either is reduced or eliminated. On some occasions, when a horse commits an infraction before it reaches the start, the judges will trigger the inquiry sign and announce that there will be a refund.

Examples of such infractions include having a horse run into another horse or racing bike; dangerously pulling out in front of another horse causing it to slow down or break; accidentally striking another horse with a whip causing it to slow down or break stride; and for failing to lose ground and pull away when the way is clear because another horse is on a break.

More on the Photo Finish

A special camera assists the judges in separating the final order of finish for horses crossing the finish line together. When the horses cannot be separated the judges will declare a *dead heat* for that finish position. More people now will be holding winning tickets. Be careful here in discarding your tickets, especially if you are holding *live* gimmick tickets. For example, if you have a 7-3-5 trifecta ticket and the 7 horse won with the 3 and 5 in a dead heat for place position, then you are entitled to receive a double payoff since you are holding a 7-5-3 as well.

Further, horses involved in the *win end* of the photo finish must stay on the track and await the outcome of the photo. Otherwise, if the horse returns to the paddock and is asked to come back to the winner's circle, the action is subject to a fine by the judges.

HOW TO READ THE TOTE BOARD:

Total amount wagered to WIN Numbers show dollars wagered on individual horses, to win.

Each horse's odds (probable payoff) for each dollar wagered. These change as public wagers more or less on each horse, and are electronically computed.

Race Number.

The "OFFICIAL" sign is posted after a review of the race finish by the Judges, and after all drivers have indicated no foul claims. Officials have photo finish camera and motion picture film patrol to aid them in decision making.

The order of finish of the top 4 horses in the previous race.

Mutuel payoffs to winners of the previous race. These prices are taken down when the horses appear on the track for the current race.

Figure 5-1: The Tote Board

24

Chapter 6

How to Behave
at the Windows

Poor etiquette at the mutuel windows and in lines waiting to wager has been a major source of irritation to both mutuel clerks and track patrons. Disappointment, distress, and anger are observed nightly when people are *shut out* at post time. But whose fault is it? The so-called professional gambler? The weekend player? The novice? The mutuel clerk? Perhaps all of the above at one time or another. Yet one thing is sure--if everyone at the track practiced some common courtesy by thinking through the wagering process fewer tempers would flare in the closing seconds before *"They're off!"*

So let's discuss the merits of learning the good manners of wagering. A thorough understanding of the etiquette of horse race wagering can save you money, lessen stress, and increase your enjoyment at the races all at the same time.

Cash Early: If you hold a winning ticket, *cash early*. Calculate your expected return beforehand, then count your payoff before you leave the window. Should there be a discrepancy, this is the time it can be remedied quickly and quietly. Don't wait until after you have returned to your seat. Once you have cashed early you can turn your full concentration to selecting the winner in the next race.

This advice is even more critical at racetracks using modern equipment which allows track patrons to cash and wager at the same window. Patrons who wait to cash and then wager at the same time, especially in the last minutes before post, may be accused of holding up the line. Because cashing often involves the counting of change, and one is encouraged to check his change before he leaves the window, it is easy to see why the window is momentarily blocked and patrons behind become impatient. Insensitive comments as that person leaves the window could have been avoided had the winning ticket been cashed earlier.

Have Your Money Ready: Nothing is more disturbing to the others in line than seeing a person at the window reach into his wallet or purse *after* the bet has been made. While it is ideal to have the exact amount of your purchase ready and in your hand, at least have your money out with all the bills facing the same way. Like clerks in a bank, mutuel personnel reduce errors and handle transactions more quickly when they don't have to take the time to sort out the bills and deposit them into the proper denomination slots.

Do not crumple up your bills or come loaded with loose change. Clerks certainly cannot be faulted for straightening out the bills to see if they are whole or altered. Nor can they be blamed for taking the time to count the silver and stack it accordingly. When a clerk is stuck with a bogus bill or insufficient funds in his till he must make up the difference out of his own pocket.

Announce Your Wager Clearly: Clerks are trained to process your wager efficiently. It helps if you follow the wagering instructions printed in the program at most tracks. Simply wait until the mutuel clerk is ready and then clearly announce your wager. Remember that it is difficult to communicate with announcements blaring over the public address system and the crowd buzzing with excitement as post time nears. Don't confuse the issue by giving your wager with a mouthful of candy or peanuts. This also applies to cigars, cigarettes, pens and pencils.

It will help, too, if you write out your wagering numbers before you reach the window. This will eliminate calling out the wrong numbers as you attempt to hurry along. Then check your ticket to see if it is correct *before* you leave the window. Should you discover that a mistake was made *after* you have left the window, do not waste time by returning to the clerk who sold you the ticket. If your case is justified, the supervisor may be able to assist you. However, this is a service not to be abused, because one is actually manipulating the odds when bets are cancelled and new ones are made.

"Wager Early and Avoid Being Shut Out": You can bet you will hear the track announcer remind the patrons in this manner at least once before each race. By betting early the track patron can avoid a major disappointment when a machine breaks down. Pari-mutuel machines, like cars, do malfunction on occasion. If this occurs, don't panic. Just be alert and move to another line.

Big bettors normally attack exotic wagering (daily double, exacta, and trifecta) buying scores of tickets. They show their consideration for the smaller player when they bet early. There is no place for fat cats with fat wallets when the public is scurrying to get their two dollars down just before post time.

Handle Your Ticket With Care: A winning ticket which has been carelessly stuffed into a pocket and, subsequently, presented to the cashier in mutilated form is a mutuel clerk's headache. It takes time to check if the ticket is, indeed, authentic.

Another bad habit to avoid is tearing up your *losing ticket* when the race is over. Occasionally, a photo finish or an interference call will change your losing ticket into a winning one when the race is declared official. If this happens to you there is a procedure to follow. Just collect the pieces of the ticket from the floor and bring them to the mutuel supervisor's window. Fortunately, these supervisors have transparent tape available for such emergencies. And if the ticket is *live* they have the authority to declare it valid. So the next time you hear the track announcer say *"Hold onto your tickets until the race is declared official,"* you will understand just what he means.

Patronize the Same Clerk: Whether you frequent the track once a day, month, or year, it pays to visit the same seller if you have confidence in him. The mutuel clerk will become use to your voice, manner and style of wagering. Ultimately, by doing business with the same clerk every time, you will reduce costly errors and increase the efficiency of the service.

Mutuel clerks need not be tipped when you cash unless they were instrumental in pointing out a specific omission in your usual style of wagering. Therefore, be honest and loyal with them at all times. If they overpay you and you fail to give them their money back, they will have to balance their tills out-of-pocket.

What to Do When:

There's a late scratch: Don't run off to exchange your ticket for a refund as you may be shut out. Instead, purchase a new ticket, then get the refund at a more opportune time.

You feel you have been shortchanged: Go right to the mutuel supervisor, explain your problem, then demand to have the window closed and cash balanced. If there is more money there than there should be, you will have won your case.

Someone behind the windows sneaks in a bet near post time: It is illegal to shut out the public in this manner, so holler and demand to be served. There is always a government official nearby to assist you in such cases.

PART TWO
Personnel

Chapter 7

Racetrack People and Places

The People in the Backstretch

Racing Secretary: This racing official is responsible for the day-to-day operations in the backstretch. He deals mainly with all the people connected with putting on a horse race, from owners to driver/trainers to judges and beyond. His task is not an easy one. The racing secretary's office staff assign stalls, check horse eligibility, and constantly communicate with horsemen. Putting the races together for the nightly ten race card is, perhaps, the racing secretary's most important function. His duties include establishing a backstretch policy, setting the conditions for each race (amount of claim or type of condition), and conducting the draw for post positions. The racing secretary strives to have the competition fair and equal in each and every race run under his supervision.

Owners: Racehorse owners are identified in the industry as horsemen. Such people come from all walks of life and have the following in common: high integrity, considerable personal investment, and a genuine love of the sport. Contrary to the belief of the uninformed track patron, horsemen are not notoriously big bettors. They depend on their share of the purse money to stay in the game. Owners, because of their substantial investments through making claims or at the horse sales, are the lifeblood of the standardbred industry.

Trainers: A trainer's prime concern is to get the horses under his care in condition to race competitively. He accomplishes this by establishing a suitable feeding and training schedule. Regular visits to the vet and for shoeing are organized by him as well. Every trainer is certified — some of the best have served a diligent apprenticeship in a successful stable which was blessed with an exceptional mechanic (trainer). A public stable of 12 horses is an ideal load for a trainer at any one time. These hard-working and talented individuals charge a daily fee for each horse in their care and normally receive 5% of each owner's share of the purse money. Unlike thoroughbred racing, harness trainers, for the most part, do their own driving as well. Only a few will hire a catch driver to do their driving for them.

Drivers: These fine athletes risk their lives and limbs every time they sit in a sulky during a race. The sport can become dangerous if a horse stumbles or breaks stride and interferes with the other horses. Therefore, uncertified or provisional drivers usually race at smaller tracks and at the fair before they get their licenses. Top drivers are said to have "good hands." They get this reputation after several years of successful and careful driving--not to mention many trips to the winner's circle. Some drivers charge a fee and normally receive 5% of the owner's share of purse money as remuneration.

Grooms: All of the best drivers and trainers started their careers as grooms. The groom's daily chores involve feeding the two or three horses in his care, harnessing each horse for his workout, cleaning out the stall, and washing and brushing down the horse after the workout. Many grooms work six-day weeks and live on the premises in tack rooms near the stalls. On race nights grooms earn extra money when they paddock their horse (harness the horse, mind it in the paddock, and then bathe it afterwards).

Veterinarian: The vet is a key individual around any racetrack. He serves the owners, trainers and racing officials in a variety of ways. Horsemen know that their horses need regular medical attention to keep sound; and track judges and stewards are relieved to have vets around when a horse becomes injured or develops a fever. The vet can scratch a horse from competition, even in the paddock, if he suspects that a horse is unsound.

The Buildings In The Backstretch

The Barns: These buildings contain the facilities necessary for the successful operation of any stable of horses: stalls, tack rooms, heat, plenty of hot and cold water, and space to harness a horse and store racing bikes or jog carts when they are not in use. Contrary to what the average track patron might think, horsemen receive stall space from raceways free of charge. But stalls are not just given away. Applications for stalls must be made to the racing secretary well before a meet begins. Depending upon the calibre of horses and the other requests for stall space, the racing secretary makes his allocations accordingly. Not all horsemen utilize this service, however. Some prefer to train their standardbreds on the farm and truck them into the track on race night.

Paddock: The paddock, always situated closest to the gate where the horses normally enter the racing surface itself, is characterized by strong security. Entry to the paddock is gained only with proper identification and upon signing in. This is where the horses stay after they complete their last major workout (approximately one hour before they go to post). Here the horses are issued their saddle cloth numbers and placed in stalls according to post position. Then, when the harness is in place, all of the equipment is checked and recorded by a paddock official.

Racing Secretary's Office: This area is where the eligibility records are stored, claims are entered, and draws for post position are conducted. Nearby, one will always find the offices of racing's regulatory bodies: the state/provincial and federal racing commissions.

The People At Trackside

Starter: This person's main function is to give all the horses a fair start. He controls the speed and release of the starting gate. In rare cases the starter declares a recall if something goes wrong near the start (interference occurs, a horse is unable to keep up with the starting gate, broken equipment is noticed, etc.). Normally, if a horse is charged with a second recall for that race, it is scratched by the starter and the betting public is permitted a refund on mutuel tickets involving the scratched horse.

Parade Marshal: Not all raceways employ the services of a parade marshal, but those who do appreciate their value. The parade marshal is recognized as the rider on horseback who leads the horses out in the post parade. Often a female, she assists the drivers if they are having difficulty controlling their horses. Sometimes she has to round up driverless horses which have gotten loose as a result of an accident.

Grounds Crew: The grounds crew, with its trucks and tractors, seems in perpetual motion around the track. Their prime function is to keep the racing surface fast. Often, after a heavy rain, they will scrape the surface down to its base to achieve this end. They brush the surface after every race to clear debris left on the track.

The Racing Track

The Surface Itself: Horsemen and track superintendents continually are looking for ways to construct a faster surface. The tartan (synthetic) composition and stonedust on spirally graded surfaces are examples of such engineering accomplishments. The spiral gradedness with its banked curves not only increases speed but also is reputed to reduce lameness in horses.

Variety of Sizes: Unlike the flats (thoroughbred racing), standardbred horses almost always race at distances of one mile. But all tracks are not of the same circumference. While most are *mile, five-eights mile,* and *half-mile,* some are 3/4 mile and 1 1/8 mile in length. The longer the track the fewer the turns (curves) a horse must negotiate. For example, over the mile distance, the number of turns vary with track size: mile (2 turns), five-eights (3 turns), and half-mile (4 turns). Thus, horses characteristically race at faster speeds on the larger tracks. Also the size of track normally dictates the number of post positions in each race. Mile tracks usually have 10 horses going to post for each race; for five-eights, it's 9; and for half-milers it's 8. It seems that when a field accommodates these numbers, then racing conditions are increasingly fair and safe.

Starting Pole: The starting pole, of necessity, is located at different places at different size tracks. The teletimer (clock) starts just after the starting gate swings open. See Figure 7-1 for an explanation of the *fair start.*

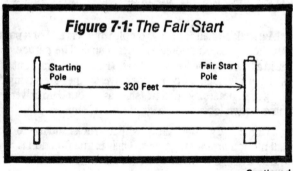

Figure 7-1: The Fair Start

Starting Pole

Fair Start Pole

320 Feet

Continued

Figure 7-1

If a horse has reached the Fair Start Pole by the time the mobile gate has reached the Starting Pole, that horse is deemed to have had a fair start. It makes no difference whether or not the horse is on or off stride at that precise moment.

THE SPEED OF THE STARTING GATE

Starting a quarter-mile away from the starting point, the mobile starting gate moves not less than 11 miles per hour for the first eighth of a mile, then not less than 18 miles per hour for the next sixteenth mile until it reaches a peak of approximately 30-35 miles per hour at the starting point depending on the quality of the horses in each particular race. A two-minute mile has an average speed of 30 miles per hour. An exceedingly fast horse under stress of keen competition could achieve a speed of 35 miles per hour for a short spurt.

Other Poles: Poles are situated along the infield near the rail at distances of 1/16 mile apart. Certain poles have distinguishable markings (1/4, 1/2, 3/4) to make them easier to recognize by drivers and the announcer. Drivers use these poles to carry out their strategy during a race. Similarly, the poles, which act as signposts, assist in the horse's training procedures before getting to the races.

Finish Line: The finish wire is suspended along the track from the finish pole at a slight angle which extends back across the track from the inside rail to a point at the outside rail. This gives the illusion that horses racing on the outside might have an advantage when crossing the finish line in a photo finish. The angle compensates for the extra distance which horses racing on the outside (parked out) have to cover. Experienced race fans have always declared the outside horse the "unofficial" winner while waiting for the results of a photo finish, but spiral graded tracks have changed that. Spiral gradedness, because of the slope in towards the inside rail, now appears to favor the inside horses in a photo finish. But we can't be certain until we see the results of the photo. See Figure 7-2 for a detailed explanation of the photo-finish camera's operation.

Figure 7-2: *How the Photo-Finish Camera Works*
The photo-finish camera, located high above the stand, has a knife-edge aperture which is placed precisely on the finish line. Thus the camera sees and records only what crosses the finish line. Film moves through the camera at approximately the same speed as the horses are travelling and produces a picture of each horse beginning at the precise moment the horse's nose reaches the finish. There are actually two cameras making a record of the finish of each race to guarantee against failure. Each horse is photographed at the exact instant his body passes the finish, no matter if he is near the inside or outside rail.

The Plant

Gates and Parking: New fans to this sport often get confused upon entering a racetrack because they are unfamiliar with the terminology regarding gates. The *Horsemen's Gate* is a pass gate for owners, trainers and other personnel employed at the raceway. The general public, or patrons as they are called, must use the other gates. Here an initial parking fee is charged. Some of the larger tracks provide preferred or valet parking, which allows one to park closer to the main building. There is a further charge for this service.

Once one approaches the main building, a decision must be made concerning where you want to sit to watch the races (grandstand, clubhouse, dining room, etc.). Admission charges are paid here, but beware of gates because you don't want to get into the wrong line.

The Building: A variety of seating is available to observe the races, and it differs from grandstand to clubhouse. Many racetracks have reserved seating which can be purchased in advance. For your convenience most racetracks also provide a coatroom for the safekeeping of your personal articles. This is a service well worth the price.

Since harness racing has become an evening sport, raceway managements have organized their buildings to suit the needs of the average fan. They want their patron to be comfortable while they are being entertained. Such buildings have suitable heating systems and many are air-conditioned. Pleasant decor, crystal clear windows, a functional public address system, and instant closed circuit television replays are examples of sincere efforts by managements to make your night at the races more enjoyable.

The People In The Plant

General Manager: The general manager is responsible for the day-to-day operation of the racetrack. His duties include overseeing the following departments: property, finance, mutuels, security, publicity, admissions, racing secretary and others. If he is not the chief executive officer he reports to the Board of Directors. Coordination, efficiency and planning are key components which normally characterize a successful GM at any raceway.

Public Relations Director: Often included in the public relations director's job description is the publicity department. His role often includes advertising, preparation of the past performance program, promotional activities and media communication. Most good PR people are creative. But, more importantly, they are successful because they are sensitive to and care for the needs of the general public.

The Announcer: Although the track announcer is remembered most for the manner in which he calls the races, his duties include more than that. More specifically, he introduces the horses during the post parade, announces changes in the program as they develop, educates the fans by providing worthwhile information about harness racing while it is happening, and, at times, is the first to alert the crowd and the grounds crew to accidents, runaway horses and potential hazards. The best announcers do their homework and make few mistakes in calling a race as it develops. If they maintain a healthy balance between a professional and entertaining approach, they are worth their weight in gold.

Judges: A judge is a person of high integrity, who has impeccable credentials and has successfully qualified for his role by passing governmental certification examinations. He is the state/provincial racing commission's representative at the raceway. During a race judges observe the conduct of drivers and horses. If they spot an infraction of the rules they cause the inquiry sign to be flashed on the tote board. And should the infraction be serious, they have the power to assess fines and suspensions. The judges declare a race official by allocating on official finish position to each horse. Sometimes, if there has been an infraction, they have the unpopular task of realigning the finish position—a decision which not only affects the bettors but also the owner's share of the purse money.

Sellers and Cashiers: As pari-mutuel machinery becomes more sophisticated both the selling and cashing transaction can be carried on at the same window. Mutuel personnel are well-trained, efficient people. They have to be because, if they make mistakes, it can cost them money out of their own pocket. Always call your bets clearly and count your change before you leave the window. Please excuse mutuel employees if they attempt to hurry you up a bit. They want to give everyone a fair chance to wager. The work of mutuel clerks is not only supervised by track management but also by the appropriate governmental department.

Security: For reasons that are quite obvious, security is especially tight around racetracks. No one, for example, can gain access to the backstretch unless he has a horseman's pass which contains his photograph. Further, entry to the paddock normally requires a pass with the horseman's signature issued by the Racing Commission. Public telephones are rarely found at a racetrack. Those raceways which do have public telephones usually make them inoperable one hour before post time. This is to detract from illegal betting and bookmaking.

Chapter 8

How a Racing Card is Put Together

Making the arrangements for a normal racing card of 10 races involving some 70-100 horses on any given night is not an easy task. Such is the lot of the racing secretary. He must not only have a sufficient number of sound horses on the grounds (or within trucking distance), but he must also know the capabilities of these horses. Owners like to have their horses race once a week to remain sharp and to earn some purse money. But, like humans, horses tend to experience ill health from time to time and require periods of rest and care. Therefore, a racing secretary at one of the larger tracks where racing is held six nights per week, usually prefers to have at least 1200 horses stabled at or near the track.

Two Categories of Horses

Basically horses at any track meeting can be separated into two catagories: *claimers* and *conditioned* horses. The former represents the lifeblood of the industry while the latter identifies the better horseflesh on the grounds.

Horses entered in the *claiming* fields have a price (dollar value) attached to their entry and may be *purchased* (claimed) by another horseman once the race is completed. Why would an owner put his horse up for sale in such fashion? Mainly because the horse has not broken down or has experienced lameness more than usual. Sometimes an owner drops his horse down into a claiming race where the competition might be less than the horse is used to. The owner assumes that he can pick up first place purse money. But, in any case, the owner knows he is risking the loss of his horse when he places a claiming price on his head. Claiming prices vary at some of the smaller tracks from $1000 to $10,000. At the larger tracks it varies from $5,000 to $20,000 and, perhaps, up to $50,000 to $100,000.

Conditioned horses, on the other hand, are sound animals which show racing promise to their owners and trainers and, therefore, are kept out of claiming races for fear of *losing* them. Traditionally these horses race against stiffer competition and for more purse money than claimers depending upon the age and stage of each horse's career. Such horses vary from *maidens* (non-winners of one lifetime start) to *open, preferred,* and *invitational* horses (which are the best and fastest at that track). They can be purchased outright in a private sale for any price agreed to when making the transaction. Ordinarily these horses are grouped together for racing purposes according to a *condition* set by the racing secretary (non-winners of so many lifetime starts or by the amount of purse money earned in a given time).

A Typical Racing Card

Any normal 10-race card (program) consists of a variety of racing talent. Often the better horses race on weekends when the crowds are larger and the purse money greater. But the racing secretary attempts to put together a *feature race* each evening for the best horses racing that night. Usually the racing secretary will sprinkle the card with some trotting races — perhaps one claimer and a conditioned race — and then he'll fill the remainder of the card with pacers.

How Conditions Are Set

It is the major responsibility of every racing secretary to ensure that the competition in each race is fair and equal. So he sets the conditions for entry into any race. Years ago when horse racing was in its infancy there were no racing secretaries per se. Hence, horses in any race were not matched fairly, resulting in lopsided victories for the *class* horses in a race. The advent of the racing secretary changed all that. Today, $5000 claimers race against other $5000 claimers and *invitational* horses race against each other.

Approximately six days before, the racing secretary *publishes the conditions for all the races on a certain race night.* These are printed and available to owners. Contained in this announcement is the closing time and date for *nominations.* An owner nominates his horse by filling out a nomination slip and placing it into the appropriate entry box.

Do note that horses sometimes are grouped together in the same race with a price value difference from $1000-$3000. In such cases, the higher priced value horses are normally assigned the outside post positions *ac-*

cording to price. Do not confuse this with *allowances* which will be explained in detail later in this section.

How Post Positions Are Drawn

When nominations are closed for a certain racing card the racing secretary will open the appropriate entry box and examine the nominations, checking to see if each meets the conditions set for the race. Once this is confirmed, he will reduce the number of horses to size (10-horse field) by any of the several accepted methods. The most common method favors those laid off from racing the longest amount of time. For instance, a horse that has not raced in 17 days will have a greater chance of drawing in than one that raced 5 days ago. Another method relies upon the discretion of the racing secretary who selects the best and discards the worst based on recent past performances. At least one horseman, representing the owners, is always present during this procedure.

The horseman's job is to witness the proceedings and participate in the draw for post positions. While post positions occasionally are drawn to price, such is not the case with most draws. The process is often handled in the following manner: post position numbers are recorded on discs and placed in one box; the nomination slips on the drawn horses are placed in another box; then on a signal the horseman simultaneously reaches in and pulls out a post position number and a nomination slip from each box. This matching of post position number and nomination slip continues until each box is empty. It should be noted that, at this time, a few additional horses, known as *also eligibles*, are selected in the event a nominated horse is scratched from the competition prior to post time. In harness racing the also eligible horse normally draws in to the position vacated by the scratched horse. Then the racing secretary records the final results of the draw for both the horsemen and for publication in the track's past performance program.

PART THREE
Horse Ownership

PART THREE

Chapter 9

All About Horse Ownership

Anyone with integrity can own a standardbred racehorse. But before you can enter your horse in a race you must become a *Horseman*. You must apply to join the federal regulatory body and pay the fee of the state or provincial racing commission in the jurisdiction where you wish to race. These bodies include the United States Trotting Association and the Canadian Trotting Association, where the fees to join each are approximately $75 per year. Racing Commission fees are $5-$10 per year.

Acquiring a Horse

The Claiming Route: Only registered horsemen can put in a claim on a horse entered in a claiming race. Cash or certified check of the claiming price must be presented at the racing secretary's office at least one hour before that horse goes postward.

Purchase Outright: Any private transaction with another horseman to acquire a horse must be properly recorded at the racing secretary's office. In addition, the horse's papers must reflect the change in ownership and be filed at the racing secretary's office as well.

At the Sales: There are several horse sales and auctions around the country which are advertised in the horseman's monthly periodicals: *Hoofbeats* (U.S.T.A.) and *Trot* (C.T.A.).

Off a Breeding Farm: One could rent a broodmare and pay the stud fees to have the mare serviced. Stud fees range from a few hundred to a few thousand dollars. This can get quite expensive if you want a proven sire of established quality. The *Meadow Skipper* stud fee is $40,000 (guaranteed live foal).

What It Costs To Own A Horse

There is no significant difference in paying the monthly training bills for a $3500 horse and another one worth $100,000. Horses normally eat the same amount of food, require the same amount of medical attention, and need the same amount of shoeing. What are these costs? Margaret Neal's breakdown, found in the September, 1979 issue of *Trot*, is detailed in Figure 9-1.

Figure 9-1:   *Horse Ownership Expenses*

		Cost per Horse/ Per Month
1.	**Training** ($20 per day at an 'A' track includes feed, conditioning, caretaking, use of jog cart, sulky use or rental)	$600
2.	**Shoeing** (one new set of shoes and one reset per month)	$ 40
3.	**Veterinary** (includes blood tests, worming, coggins tests, liniments and supplements — all necessary for a healthy horse. Costs multiply if the horse does not stay sound)	$100
4.	**Equipment Replacement and Repair** (replacement of incidentals such as bell boots, muffs, blankets, leg wraps, bandages, laundry costs)	$50-75
5.	**Equipment — Initial outfitting —** **($600-$1,000)** (This comprises anything the horse wears or uses — harness, blankets, tack box, hopples, bits, brushes, towels, feed tubs, water pails. If harness is replaced yearly, figure an additional annual $250 expense)	$50-85
6.	**Insurance** (Assuming horse is valued at $25,000, cost of full mortality insurance is calculated at approximately $4 per $1,000. Cost would be $100 per year)	$8.50

Continued

Figure 9-1

7.	**Stakes payments** (For moderately staked campaigner which might race the Ontario Sires Stakes circuit and perhaps four other events — Total $1,000)	$ 85
8.	**Transportation** (Based on 2,000 miles to ship for OSS and other stakes events, at approximately 50 cents per mile, or a total $1,000)	$ 85
9.	**Incidentals** (Border crossings, CTA, USTA, ORC and state commission licenses will probably total $100 or more)	$ 10
	Basic Expenses — Per Month — $ 1,025-$ 1,085 Per Annum — $12,300-$13,020	
10.	**Other Expenses** (Driver-trainer's share of purse earnings is a traditional 10 percent, but also figure the cost of paying a groom to paddock the horse on race nights, and you can plan to part with 12 to 15 percent of your horse's earnings. To cover basic expenses, you'd better pay to be in the money — often.)	

All things considered, it costs about $12,000 to keep a standardbred racehorse. Therefore, if an owner wants to break even, his horse must earn at least $12,000 in purse money each year.

Privileges of Ownership: Perhaps the best privilege is having your picture taken in the winner's circle after a win. But there are other privileges too. Each owner gets two clubhouse passes and overnight passes on days when his horse races. He's entitled to free parking and entrance to the paddock. Whenever he visits a harness track out of town he can get free parking and clubhouse passes by contacting the racing secretary's office at that track.

Getting the Horse to the Race

Philosophy: Standardbreds in North America traditionally start racing as two year olds if they are ready. In Australia, however, horsemen generally wait until the horse is four or five before they get it to the races. The lucrative Sire Stakes programs for two and three year olds on this continent is, no doubt, the reason for early entry into the racing scene. Not all horses are ready to race at two or three, however, so their owners wait an extra year or two. Some are unsound and time is needed for bones to grow stronger; others simply need more schooling. Now let's examine how a trainer gets his horse ready for the big test — his first qualifier.

Training the Yearling: No matter what time of year foals are born they all celebrate their first birthday the following January on New Year's Day. On New Year's Day horses born in the year prior become yearlings. Breeders give these yearlings time and space to grow, providing suitable food and medical attention. Such breeding operations want these yearlings to be in the best possible health when the "Select Yearlings Sales" and horse auctions occur in the fall of each year.

Trainers usually begin to "work" with their yearlings as soon as they bring them home from the sales. The yearling's training and schooling progresses through a series of steps: first comes the introduction to bridle and bit; next the yearling is line driven (led around with a lead rope and trailed by a second person holding the reins); third, the colt or filly is hitched to a training bike; and fourth, the yearling is schooled in developing good manners around other horses, in the stall, while shoeing, when being harnessed, and with trainers and grooms. The entire process can take from a few weeks to a few months.

By early January, the horse turns two and is normally ready to formally begin training for its freshman year of racing. Some jogging, while hitched to a training bike, already has begun where the horse is jogging two to three miles per day. The trainer likes to get his young two year old jogging a training mile in close to three minutes at some time in January. He intends to step up his training schedule by shaving about 10 seconds off the training mile each month until the horse is ready for his first qualifier.

When a two year old is jogging a training mile around 2:10 - 2:20, more schooling takes place. Then the colt or filly is trained regularly with other horses: learning to follow (remain tucked in line behind the other horses); firing (moving out ahead alongside the other horses) when called upon to improve position; and tucking in on the rail or taking the lead when directed by the trainer's reins. And, finally, when the trainer thinks his horse is ready, practice will be given behind a starting gate. Shortly thereafter, the two year old prepares to enter his first qualifier. If the horse meets the time standard in the qualifier that is set by the racing secretary for young horses, then the horse can be entered in his first pari-mutuel race.

Horsemen Who Bet Must Follow Rules

While many horsemen are content to reap their financial rewards through earning purse money, some occasionally wager on their own horse. This is part of the fun of owning a horse. Horsemen can go to the mutuel windows and wager like any other track patron on any race where their own horse is not participating. But when one's own horse is competing in a race, the horseman who wishes to wager must adhere to certain rules.

It's legitimate to wager on your own horse, but it is considered *illegal* to bet *against* one's own horse. Therefore, it is considered a break of trust if an owner, driver, trainer or groom wagers on any horse other than his own in a race where any of the above have a horse competing. In exacta or trifecta races where they have an entry, horsemen may wager only on combinations where their horses are placed *on top* (in the *win* position). Furthermore, horsemen are prohibited from using their own horse for second or third in feature wagering. These special wagering rules protect the public and discourage *hanky panky* among horsemen.

Qualifying Races: The racing secretary has the right to refuse an entry into a race on a horse which he believes would not be competitive. Such horses are made to *qualify* before they can be entered into a pari-mutuel race. Qualifying races are *non-betting* and usually held twice a week, either in the afternoon or just before first post on some nights. These races are designed to determine a horse's ability to perform within standards prescribed by a particular track. The racing secretary is responsible for establishing the qualifying standards. Normally, a horse which has broken stride in his last two races is asked to qualify before its next start. Similarly, horses are required to qualify if they were *distanced* in their last race, or if they have been away from the races an exceptionally long time (usually 30 days or more).

Stakes Races: Horsemen consider *added money* races like *stakes races* and *futurities* as the more prestigious horse races. Such races, however, require both a *nomination* and one or more *stakes payments* before the race is held. Often such horses are nominated during their first year of birth and payments continue from that time until the horse is withdrawn from the race or actually entered for competition. All payments are usually added to the purse money for the event. Stakes and futurities are limited almost exclusively to two and three year-old horses. Since breeding operations have expanded significantly, with new owners nominating more and more of their young stock, it is no wonder that some of these stakes races have purse money valued at one million dollars or more. The Woodrow Wilson Pace and the Meadowlands Pace come to mind.

Horsemen and Drugs: Regulations governing the use of drugs vary from state to state and from province to province. Horses that are racing must not be given drugs which are on the *prohibited list* at a racetrack. Furthermore, if certain prohibited drugs are in the possession of anyone in the backstretch and are detected, then criminal prosecution and/or penalties could be imposed. A horseman takes a serious risk (loss of license or fine) if he uses drugs as a stimulant to make his horse perform better. It may not come as a surprise that after every race a specific procedure relating to illegal drug detection takes place. Often the race winner and one or more other horses selected at random undergo blood and/or urine tests. Sometimes the governing agency will camp right in the paddock and test every horse before the race.

Age and Eligibility Restrictions: Horses can be raced in pari-mutuel races from the time they are two year olds until they reach age fifteen. Horses must retire from active competition when they are fifteen, but are still permitted to run at the fairs after that. Some raceways even hold Retirement Paces on New Year's Eve for 14-year-old horses.

The C.T.A. outlines specific eligibility requirements. The youngest age at which a horse is permitted to race is two years — with age reckoned from January 1 of the year of the foaling. In addition to meeting registration requirements, a horse must be tattooed and an "eligibility certificate" must have been issued for the horse before it is eligible to start in any race. A lip tattooing system is used in North America to identify trotters and pacers. In Canada, it is administered by CSHS which schedules

56

tattoo technicians' visits to tracks, training centers and farms. The "eligibility certificate" is a document which establishes the identity and eligibility of a horse for racing purposes and upon it are recorded the detailed performance lines of each start of the horse, regardless of the type of race involved. Should a horse appear for a race without an eligibility certificate, the horse would not be permitted to race.

Modern day computer technology is providing raceways with more efficiency than ever before. For example, most of the larger racetracks are hooked into a computer which permits them to check a new horse's eligibility even before the horse arrives. This service becomes particularly useful to the department responsible for printing the past performance program. Thus, the entry can be printed even before the eligibility certificate is presented for approval to the racing secretary.

The Winner's Circle

Next to owning a racehorse the biggest thrill is getting that first win and having your picture taken in the Winner's Circle. Track patrons in the stands and clubhouse often wonder just who is in the Winner's Circle after a race. The owner, his family, the trainer and the groom are usually present for the picture-taking ceremony. In addition, the owner may invite friends or guests to accompany him. When the race is a special event and a blanket or trophy is to be presented, either an official from the raceway or sponsoring agency makes the presentation. The owner gets to keep the blanket or, in the case of the trophy, a replica for both practical and sentimental purposes. Contrary to what one might think, the owner usually must pay for the photograph once it is developed.

Forming A Stable

Although many owners prefer to own their horses outright, some like to take in partners to share the investment. All partners must become registered and certified horsemen. Normally, when four or more partners own a horse, a *stable* must be formed. This regulation is fairly consistent throughout North America.

For business purposes, some stables incorporate while others do not. Members of a stable which has not incorporated can enjoy certain tax benefits from year to year; while those who have incorporated enjoy the legal protection that comes with becoming incorporated. Be advised that horse ownership is not the tax write off it once may have been. A few can still qualify as farmers in some locales, thereby receiving certain taxable allowances, but many still get into the sport as a hobby.

Leasing A Horse

Occasionally a track patron will open his program and notice that a horse has been *leased* from an owner. Now, why would any owner want to lease his horse to someone else? This situation often occurs when a current racing meet ends and the horses are required to leave the grounds for a considerable distance (200 miles or more). An owner wants to keep his horse sound and racing, but is unable to make the travel commitment that is required. So the owner decides to lease his horse—usually to a trainer—thereby reducing costs.

A lease contract is customarily drawn up which specifies the agreement according to care, training, feed, shoeing, vet bills, trucking and purse shares. In exchange for a high percentage of future purse monies, the lessee usually agrees to pick up all the other expenses. If the horse is a claimer, then the lessee is given permission to race the horse within a certain price range. However, if the horse is claimed, the claiming price (money used in the purchase) reverts to the owner and not the lessee unless otherwise stipulated in the agreement.

Occasionally a trainer will lease a horse he has left behind to another trainer when he moves to a track with higher calibre horses. Such a horse, perhaps, is not in shape yet or is just not good enough to race in the minimum class at the new track. When these horses are ready the lessee will enter them in races where the competition is equal to their expected performance.

WINNER'S PURSE

Chapter 10

So You Want to be a Horse Owner

Getting into harness racing as an owner can be a very expensive proposition. There are so many ways to lose money as an owner that you really have to know what you are doing if you are to end up with a profit. Let me give you the benefit of my experience as an owner. It could save you thousands of dollars.

I have owned thirteen horses. These included *Patty Tar, Famed Yankee, Muddy Don, Cedarwood Sam, Faster Master, Calton Hill, Miss Dottie Seton, Tricky Rhythm, Romeo Lee, Tigalus, Tuff Buck, Stephen Direct N,* and *Triangle Boy.*

I got into horse owning in 1973 with four other guys. We decided to throw in a thousand dollars each and claim a horse for $5000. There was Andy the doctor, Jerry the planner, Walter the cabinetmaker, Ed the personnel man, and me, the professor/gambler. I had been going to the races since the early 1960s and was the most knowledgeable of the group about the horses. I was appointed to find a horse.

Since I was going to the races every night, I had all the programs. I went through them all looking for a horse that was fairly young and that was winning races recently, despite being owned by a relatively unknown trainer and being driven by one of the poorer drivers.

At the same time, we approached the racetrack management to help us find a trainer. They spread the word around the backstretch that there were some new people wanting to get into the horse racing business. One of the trainers who was looking for new owners at that time was Phil Hinks. We invited Mr. Hinks to meet us at the doctor's house to talk things over.

---

¹This chapter is taken from the book *Harness Racing Gold* by Igor Kusyshyn, Ph.D., International Gaming Inc., 1979.

At the meeting I showed him the latest program in which a horse I had my eye on, called *Patty Tar,* had won her last race. *Patty Tar* was a four year-old mare who was winning a whopping one-third of her races. For some reason the trainer/driver was keeping her in the same class. Mr. Hinks looked at the program and agreed that she would probably be a good claim. So a few days later, on a cold winter evening at Greenwood Raceway, we claimed her for $5000.

The horse turned out to be a very successful claim. She made over $10,000 for us in less than twelve months. Then she was claimed from us for the same price for which we had claimed her. Thus, we got our purchase price back, made enough to pay for the training costs, and netted a profit of just over $5000. I really liked the profit part.

Weekly at the doctor's house we had lengthy talks about how the horse did in her last race, how she should be handled for the next race, whether Mr. Hinks was handling her properly, what class she should be racing in next time, and so on and on and on.

After the first few meetings I became bored and frustrated. I thought Mr. Hinks was doing a good job. We were winning races and finishing in the money in almost every race. Mr. Hinks got the horse up to race as high as $7000 claiming. And so far as I could see, there was no reason to have all these meetings.

A couple of the guys, however, weren't satisfied with the way Mr. Hinks was handling the horse. They wanted him to socialize more. They wanted to have more meetings with him to discuss the horse and to learn more about horseracing. As I learned later, most trainers do not have the time or the inclination to spend a lot of time with their owners. Training is a job to them and it is a serious job—it's their source of livelihood—and most of them do the best they can to get the most out of the horse for their owners.

To make a long story short, at the time the horse was claimed there was disagreement within our group on how to proceed. In fact, there had been a vote in which it was decided to make a change to another trainer. One of the guys had located a young, inexperienced man, with an unproven record, who was a-friend-of-a-friend of the doctor's. I didn't want any part of this transfer but the others were set on it. I wrote Mr. Hinks a letter afterwards to say that, as far as I was concerned, he was doing a great job and explained that I had no part in the decision to replace him.

After that first experience I decided not to get involved with a lot of other owners on my next horse. Luckily, one of the boys I went to school with bought a farm with his father, built a training track on the farm, and started to learn how to train horses. Within just a few years they became high-quality trainers.

The next horse I claimed was in partnership with these two, Dave and Dennis (father and son respectively). The horse was *Muddy Don*. We claimed *Muddy Don* for $7500, and Dennis and Dave developed him to the point where he was winning $20,000 claiming races. He was a very successful horse and is still racing.

Unfortunately, Dave recently decided to get out of the training business because it was too cold and demanding in the winter. And Dennis wanted to shift out of training and racing and into breeding. He has had, in fact, a very successful sale of his first crop of yearlings. But, as a result, I had to find other trainers. By this time I had several other horses and we raced them at the Meadowland Race Track in East Rutherford, New Jersey.

I had some very bad luck with two New Zealand horses that I bought with Leonard Boyd, my new trainer. One of them cost $50,000— $30,000 of which was my share. The other one we bought for $20,000. These two purchases taught me a very important lesson. Never buy a horse, always claim one. A claimed horse is one that has already proven what he can do. A purchased horse may be unproven even though well bred. The two New Zealand horses were unproven on this continent.

Both horses took months and months to get acclimatized to North America and to adjust to North American racetracks. One of them is now winning races in classes much lower than his original price. The other one had one race (in which he ran ninth) in six months. He just does not want to race even though there doesn't seem to be anything wrong with him. His name is *Faster Master*. I suspect a more appropriate name would be *Slower Slave*. It was an expensive lesson.

Rules for Claiming

1) The first rule is to claim a horse out of a race that is already proven. Never buy a horse that is unproven. I paid out $40,000 for two unproven horses and have regretted it ever since. I was sold on these horses by the trainer who felt they were good buys. He genuinely believed that the

horses were worth that kind of money. Unfortunately, he was mistaken.

When you claim a horse you are claiming it out of a race for a specific price and you already know how well the horse races at that price. You know whether he was winning or coming second, or fifth or tenth in the class. There is no need to guess how good the horse is or to hope that he will be able to win in some high class.

2) The second factor you should keep in mind is age. The horse should be between three and six years of age. A horse that is only three years old may be a bit risky as a claim because he is not fully developed and already may have injured himself through the strain of racing. However, if the horse has been lightly raced (if he's only had a dozen or so lifetime races), then it is not very probable that the horse will have been injured.

The horse should not be older than six because by then you run a sizable risk of getting a *second-hand horse*. This is a horse that has already sustained injuries and may even have had some operations on his legs. Some of these horses do go on to race, and make money, but it is just a matter of time before they slow down or break down. In the latter case, you'll lose your purchase price as I did with 11-year-old *Tigalus*. When I claimed *Tigalus* he was winning half of his races! I claimed him for $5500. The next week he won $6500 at Windsor Raceway. Tragically, the second week at Windsor he broke a leg and had to be carted off in a horse ambulance. The lesson cost me $4500. Never claim an old horse, even if he was once an Invitation horse.

3) Sex is the third aspect. It is preferable to claim a gelding rather than a male horse or a filly or mare. The reason is that geldings keep their minds on the races and are more consistent than fillies, mares, or stallions.

Fillies and mares tend to get moody at certain times of the year and are less consistent then. Mares seem to race better in the cold weather. Horses do get sexually aroused and can get quite hyperactive and act up before a race. This unnecessary hyperactivity can diminish their interest in racing and can also create unnecessary tension in the horse.

4) The fourth point to consider is price. How much should you pay for the horse? I recommend that the absolute minimum be $7500. I have found that the few horses I claimed for smaller amounts have either just

managed to pay for themselves or lost money. With inflation pushing up the price of everything you have to have a horse who can run for decent purses in order to cover your costs. The absolute minimum should be $7500 but, in fact, you should be looking at $10,000 and, even better, $15,000 as the lowest price bracket.

Fifteen thousand dollar claimers run for purses of at least $3000 at most racetracks in North America. If they are consistent, in that they run in the money in most of their races, then they will not only pay for themselves but actually show profit for you as an owner.

5) Fifth is win percentage. The horse you claim should have at least a 16% win percentage. In other words, he should be winning at least once in every six starts. The average horse at the track wins at about this rate and you want a horse who is at least average. I have seen some atrocious claims, where horses were claimed that only won one or two races in twelve months. Very rarely do such horses improve after they are claimed. Some horses don't like to win races. They're very happy coming second, third, or eighth. Others have more courage, heart, guts, or whatever you want to call it and they want to win every time. This is the kind of horse you want to claim.

6) The sixth question is who should you claim from? This is a very important criterion. It is best to claim a horse from a relatively unknown trainer who stables his horses at the racetrack instead of on a farm. The reason for doing this is that your trainer, who should be one of the better trainers at the racetrack, will have a better chance to improve the horse's performance once he has claimed it. The reason why it is important to claim a horse that is stabled at the track is that it is difficult to improve on horses that have been kept on a farm.

7) The next thing to worry about is the quality of your trainer. Ideally, you want a trainer whose horses show a high win percentage. However, it is not ideal to have one of the most popular trainers at the track. That would be your second choice.

Your first choice should be a trainer who only trains and does not drive. Training and driving both are very demanding on any one individual. It is also important to pick a trainer who has up to a dozen horses in his stable and no more. In this way he can give very personal attention to each of his horses.

A number of the top trainers in North America have stables of 30, 50, 100, and even 200 horses. Unless they get very good assistant trainers and conscientious grooms to look after all those horses it is simply impossible for them to give the care to your horse that another trainer with fewer horses can give.

8) The eighth point is the farm. Ideally your trainer should have his own farm on which he can keep the horses between races. Horses love to roam in the fields and eat green grass. Several trainers have told me that a horse "raced off the farm" can gain as much as one second (that's five lengths) over horses that are stabled at the track. Since most races are won by three lengths or less, you can see that a difference of one second can be critical if you intend to make money as an owner.

9) Rule number nine is that before claiming a horse make sure that he is sound. In fact, few of them are. Most horses have some kind of lameness to some degree. The best you can hope for is to get a horse that is what the trainers call *racetrack sound*. That is, a horse sound enough to race.

Before you claim, you should ask around in the backstretch about the horse you're interested in. Find out from a groom who has worked with the horse, from a former owner, or possibly from a veterinarian who has worked on the horse whether there is anything seriously wrong with him.

However, you have to be discreet about how you go about getting this information, because if the current owner of the horse finds out that someone is interested in him he may well put the horse up several thousand dollars in claiming price. That's the price you'll have to pay for being snoopy.

10) The tenth point is the horse's gait and appearance. Although this is not as important as the other points, you should check to see that he has good conformation. Does he have a large chest for good lung capacity? In addition, he should have a nice smooth gait. Does he run smoothly in the race, especially around the curves? It is also good if your horse doesn't have to wear any kind of special equipment such as a special bit, two head poles, a mask or bandages. The less equipment your horse wears, the less temperamental he is likely to be.

11) The final criterion is natural class. Natural class is reflected in the horse's breeding. A book of Sires and Dams lists the best and worst sires and dams. Available for about $10 from the United States Trotting Association, this is a very valuable book to have. At least one of your horse's two parents should have shown above average speed or have produced speedy horses.

These are the rules you should use if you want to survive financially as an owner. Good luck!

Chapter 11

All About Claiming

The "buying and selling" of horses via the claiming route adds to the excitement of horse racing. This swirl of activity by horsemen represents the lifeblood of the industry. It enables the smaller stables to compete equally for the purchase of horseflesh with the larger stables at any raceway. The average racing fan really knows very little about the procedures and regulations governing claiming. So let's look into this integral part of the racing scene.

Pre-Race Inspection: Once the owners have signed the claiming declaration form and entered their horse in a claiming race, the speculation begins. Prospective claimants may visit the stable area a day or two before to inspect the horses. Often these potential owners will sit in the stands and observe the horse working out. Presumably, something good about the horse has caught their eye already (seeing his last race or from the past performance program). Nevertheless, the prospective claimant usually believes he can improve that horse's performance so he wants to be sure of the horse's physical condition before he puts his money into the claiming box.

How Claims Are Made: The regulations governing claiming are quite similar in both the United States and Canada. All that the prospective claimant has to do is fill out a claim form indicating the name of the horse, place the form and a certified check or cash in an envelope, seal the envelope, write the date, race number and track name on the front of the envelope, and then present it to the racing secretary's designate at least 30 minutes prior to post time for that horse.

Only persons eligible to make a claim are allowed this privilege. Such eligible persons include owners (or lessees), drivers, trainers, or authorized agents. At the completion of the race, the new owner of the horse takes over. The horse is his, regardless. The previous owner, however, is entitled to receive any purse money which the horse earned during the race.

Questions Often Asked About Claiming

What happens when more than one claim is made on the same horse?
The judges draw lots at the conclusion of the race and then immediately announce the result to the paddock judge.

Can a prospective claimant withdraw his claim?
No! Once the envelope containing a claim has been submitted it cannot be withdrawn.

Can an owner scratch his horse to avoid it being claimed?
Not really! If such a scratched horse is entered in any other race within the next 30 days, regardless of the conditions, a claim can be made on that horse at the previous claiming price—unless the next race is a claimer at even lower claiming prices.

Why the secrecy with the sealed envelopes?
Basically, for the protection of the new owner. Sometimes drivers have been accused of taking unnecessary risks with their horses if they knew they would lose them after a race. In former times when horse racing was not as rigidly supervised, claimed horses were, on occasion, delivered to their new owners bruised and bleeding. Today, however, such behavior would necessitate fines and possible suspension by the judges.

Chapter 12

Keeping a Horse Sharp

Philosophy: In general, standardbred race horses need to race every week to 10 days to maintain their sharpness. From an economic point of view, this is necessary because owners will want to pick up some purse money to help pay their bills. Two or three times a year, however, it is wise to give a horse a change of scenery on a farm where the horse is "turned out to pasture" for a 2-3 week period. After that, training begins again and normally the horse can be ready to race in a week or two after the rest.

The Week Before: A horse which has been racing regularly (every 7-10 days) is given a set pattern of workouts by his trainer days before his next race to maintain condition. Usually the horse is given a hard training mile three to four days prior to race night. Customarily, the hard workout session is followed with some light jogging each day (3-6 miles). Then the day before the race night the horse is blown out—trained quickly again, but not as hard as two or three days before. Pre-race medication and examination may be administered by the trainer's veterinarian during these days.

On Race Night: Trainers get their horse onto the track three or four times before post time of their actual race: the first is traditionally two hours before post time; the second is one hour before post; and the third is in the post parade where the horses and their drivers are introduced about eight minutes before the race.

The initial warmup, two hours prior to post, consists of light jogging (2-3 miles) which is intended to loosen up the horse a bit. Normally the horse is jogged the opposite way (clockwise) around the track, keeping to the outside away from the rail. Please note that trainers must conform to certain rules at the track to avoid accidents since several horses may be running in opposite directions. Those trainers jogging their horses must go in a clockwise direction and keep to the *outside*, while those running a workout mile run in the counterclockwise direction (racing direction) and stay to the *inside* (near the rail).

Next, the *main warmup* or workout, as it is sometimes called, occurs about one hour before the horse goes postward. When the horse comes out here he is, at times, jogged for ½ mile or so first. But traditionally the trainer turns the horse the right way (counterclockwise) and works a full mile simulating what he wants the horse to do later on in the actual race. This workout is several seconds slower than competitive speed, but it gives the trainer a good idea of how the horse will perform that night. If you are particularly observant at this time you can see many of the trainers begin to urge their horses to go faster just past the final 3/8 pole, gradually asking the horse to increase his speed, as he would in a race, to the finish line.

Approximately 90% of all horses are trained in the manner just described, one hour prior to post. This *training mile*, as it is also named, exhibits a horse's physical attributes and may tip off a horse's condition to both the trainer and fans in the stands. These alert fans are known around the track as *clockers,* and can be recognized as having a stopwatch in one hand and a pencil plus clipboard in the other.

Some horses are not turned onto the track for their warmup. A few work out on the practice track if one is available. The reasons for this difference in warmup procedure vary. Such horses may be lame or the trainer may wish to conserve his horse's energy for the actual race.

Finally, the horse participates in a light final warm up about eight minutes before post—just after the horse is announced in the post parade. Here you will observe the horses warm up further. Some are jogged lightly, while others are walked slowly in the opposite direction keeping close to the fence.

The warmup activity described in the preceding paragraphs explains the reason for so many horses on the track between races. It serves as an opportunity for the track patron to have an early look at the horses before he wagers. This is why all the horses can be identified by their saddle cloth colors and numbers. Consult your past performance program or that area where the color code is painted on the rail near the finish line to match up race numbers and colors on the horses warming up.

PART FOUR
Harness Handicapping

Chapter 13

Handicapping Fundamentals

The purpose of this book is to introduce you to the exciting sport of harness racing. People, horses, machines, buildings, and property all play an integral part. But handicapping is the one activity which draws millions of people to the tracks around the country every year. Selecting a horse in condition to win from a number of contenders sums up all that is the science of handicapping.

Handicapping: Exploring and Exploding the Myths

The following dialogue has been reproduced in part from *Stanley's Law: A Textbook About Selecting Winners at the Harness Races*. Al Stanley, popular full-time professional handicapper/author, explodes some of the myths connected with handicapping the harness races.

The average racing fan knows very little about the harness racing industry itself. But if you talk to anyone who attends the races with any regularity he will try to convince you he is an "authority." He can offer all kinds of "explanations" as to why a particular horse won or didn't win a race. Unfortunately, this misinformed fan continues to perpetuate some of the myths that have been damaging to horse racing for years.

Let's investigate why this happens. The average fan loses much more than he wins; chances are that he sits beside losers, is surrounded by losers, and is influenced by what they say when they lose. Also, he tends to overreact to media sensationalism concerning the rare scandal in the sport. What he fails to do is check out what he hears with a legitimate source. Horsemen (drivers, trainers, and owners), harness publications, and, yes, even professional handicappers are valid sources of information about harness racing.

Al, are races really "fixed" like so many people will lead you to believe?

Absolutely not! There are always a few bad apples in every barrel. Government regulations are so strict and enforcement so sophisticated today that the "cheaters" are exposed and dealt with accordingly. Besides, horsemen have far too much to lose if they are caught—purse money, their licenses, their membership in standardbred associations, and their reputations. I am a horse owner and sincerely believe that there are not as many fixed races as there are plane crashes. And if you know anything about statistics, plane travel is the safest mode of transportation known to man.

If I thought that the majority of races were fixed or that there was a lot of cheating going on I wouldn't be near the racetrack. As a horse owner, I am often in the company of drivers, trainers and other owners. I have found them to be very honest, sincere and dedicated people—not the type to risk their reputations or their livelihoods in this fashion.

I see so many patrons at the track consulting scratch sheets and the newspaper picks to assist them in their handicapping. How good are these public selectors?

Some are very good but, basically, they are unreliable. Nevertheless, they are responsible for making the odds in most cases. These people are not experts. In fact, many do not even attend the races on a regular basis. You will often see four of them pick four different "winners" in the same race. So you can see how easy it is for the fan to become confused. Most of the horses they give you end up being chalk (the favorite) anyway. I do not put any faith in public selections of any kind.

The average fan usually stays with one factor when handicapping. Is this advisable?

No! One-factor handicappers go broke. You must use a variety of factors to be a successful handicapper.

People are basically lazy. They will not admit that, nor will they admit that they do not have the knowledge to select good winners. It's human nature. So many people rely on one-factor handicapping and you have heard them all: whether it be the speed of the horse, the horse with the best post position, the horse with the biggest "move" in his last race. Regardless, they stick to one factor only and this is wrong. Predicting the outcome of races consistently depends on how well you take a number of factors and put them together to pick winners over a period of time.

I have heard many track patrons say that Lady Luck plays a great part in whether or not one is a winner at the races.

Nonsense! Nobody is consistently lucky or consistently unlucky. One does not need luck when one possesses knowledge and utilizes sound handicapping basics when making selections.

I see a lot of patrons and gamblers at the track getting tips and being touted. Are these people with "information" making money?

First of all, I personally believe that anyone who does "know" something certainly wouldn't be telling anybody about it. I don't pay any attention to "information"—it interferes with my handicapping.

Legitimate tips are few and far between. It's an ego trip for most people. They think they know something and feel compelled to share it with others. You are much better off doing your own selecting. If you listen to tips you will go broke in a hurry.

You are a horse owner. Have you ever given out tips on your horses?

Yes, absolutely! It is human nature to want to share your "good news" with others, especially when you first get into the business. You really do feel you have inside information and it's a matter of an ego trip again. So you will tout someone if they ask you, especially if you and your trainer felt that the horse's chances of winning were good. If he's in shape and "ready" you will want to pass the information along. But I do not pass information on anymore—too many disappointments. And horsemen tend to overestimate their horse's chances anyway.

Many people at the track believe that owners and trainers cash the really big tickets. Is this true?

Some horsemen are more successful than others, but, generally, they "cannot see the forest for the trees." As I said earlier, they tend to overestimate their own horses and simply forget to look at the other horses in the race. Even when signs of condition show up they fail to recognize it because their minds have already been made up as to their horse's chances.

A case in point happened in Windsor a couple of years ago. I had clocked a super warmup. The driver/trainer (who was also the owner) was simply flat in his bike trying to keep his horse under control. Although the horse was making a small drop in class and in his last race was the beaten favorite, the public allowed him to go off at 25-1. Of course, he "won for fun" as horsemen say. And lo and behold, when I approached the owner after the races he said he hadn't bet a dime. His explanation was understandable. He figured the bad post position was too much to overcome and that the horse might get into trouble. Here the owner had *underestimated* his horse.

From my experience this is how the majority of the people in the backstretch operate. They don't know when they have a "good thing." These people wager at the wrong time, losing their money, then when they really need it to wager they do not have any money left.

"Hey! That driver didn't try at the end! Did you see how he 'stiffed' his horse (held him back)?" Al, what is your reaction to the upset public when you hear such catcalls after a race?

This situation occurs frequently near the end of a harness race to a horse which has expended an unusual amount of energy during the race. What the fan "appears" to see is a horse being held back in the final yards, especially if he thinks the horse may have finished first or second.

In reality, the driver is trying to hold the horse together. The horse has been "all out" (extended) earlier in the race and is tiring. When this happens a horse veers out and heads away from the rail. The driver realizes he has the horse's weight to control and is just trying to keep his horse from falling down while still attempting to pick up the best part of the purse that he can. It is absolute folly to believe that a driver, trainer or owner would throw away purse money, especially the front end of a purse! Does it make sense to you?

For your information, purse money is usually distributed as follows:

First place finish	-	50% of purse
Second place finish	-	25% of purse
Third place finish	-	12% of purse
Fourth place finish	-	8% of purse
Fifth place finish	-	5% of purse

(Drivers and trainers generally *each* receive 5% of the owner's share of the purse.)

Often, too, at the final eighth or sixteenth pole of a race, we notice that the "rail opens" for one of the trailing horses and the crowd becomes angry. Can you explain this?

I can see that people would want to know why the driver in the lead would let a horse in on the rail—the one that beat him. The fans just fail to realize how difficult it is for a driver to direct a horse that outweighs him tremendously. Most successful drivers are light people (averaging 130-150 lbs.), which shows that weight is a significant factor in harness racing.

Now to answer your question. What is happening is this: That horse has been out front (which is hard work) and is tiring with about a sixteenth of a mile to go. And when a horse tires he veers out to the right (outside). Now picture a light driver trying to keep him going in a straight line. It's an impossibility. He actually has no control over the horse at this point, so the horse veers out and, as a result, the rail opens. Behind him we have a "live horse" that perhaps has had a "perfect trip" who just shoots up and wins the photo. That is unfortunate. The driver has done the best he can. The horse was all out and he didn't have anything left, so he just couldn't stay in a straight line.

Another comment I hear from the "losers" at the track is "Gee, that driver didn't even use the whip on the horse." Are such complaints valid?

Not all horses can be whipped. Many of them are "sulkers." If you start whipping sulkers they'll go backwards or even stop altogether. On the other hand, stallions (those listed as 'H' under 'sex' in the program) are stubborn and often need to be whipped from start to finish.

I have witnessed a race where a new driver had started to whip his horse into the final eighth and the horse actually stopped on the track. We even owned a young horse once who stopped when the trainer whipped him because he thought that he was doing something wrong and that the trainer was displeased. Similarly, I have observed a trainer whipping his horse in the backstretch and the horse wouldn't even lift up his foot to move.

Horses, like people, can get very stubborn and will not respond under certain conditions. Drivers have to handle sulkers differently. If the horse is close to the finish line and has a chance to get in the money, the driver must carefully "hand ride" the horse and coax him to the wire. The driver might just as well have left his whip in the barn because he knows if he uses it he has no chance at all.

I have heard many fans argue that it really does not matter how "lucky" you are at the races because the track will grind you down. The track's legal take of 18-20% will eventually absorb all of your money.

I do not agree with that and have an answer for those who say the track will grind you down. I say to them that if I bet $10,000 over a meet and take from the cashiers' windows, $14,000, then I have made $4,000 profit.

Let's get back to handicapping. Is class the separater, the ultimate divider that many people claim it is?

No, that's not true at all. Nevertheless, most fans, horsemen, and public selectors will have you believe otherwise. I guess class would be if there was no racing secretary to keep the competition properly aligned. What used to happen years ago, before the rating systems came into existence, was that you could have a $20,000 claimer racing against a $2,500 claimer. In such cases, class would win out all the time.

That doesn't happen today. Races are made up so that $5,000 claimers race against other $5,000 claimers; or the horses are matched by the total purse money they have earned over either a specified period of time or number of starts. Ordinarily the horses are evenly matched and, indeed, difficult to separate. Yet, horsemen will still feel that class is the ultimate factor in handicapping. They blindly say that if a horse is dropping down in class, neither a horse's condition nor his speed has any bearing. They'll take the horse which is dropping down. As an example, perhaps the horse raced a year ago in invitational company and today he's racing in a $20,000 claimer. They feel that his former "class" will be good enough to win the race.

This is not so! These horsemen will continue to favor what they call "the best bred in the stretch." However, I cannot find any statistics to consistently substantiate that belief. As a matter of fact, it is exactly the opposite. Most of the horses that are well bred do not even get to the races. Less than 10% of the high-priced horses from breeding farms actually win pari-mutuel races. So you can see why class is *not* the ultimate separater for me.

Lastly, what have you to say to those racing fans who claim that all handicapping systems are bad?

While I agree that most systems are bad, a few of them are good. Unfortunately, the bad systems are published by "hit and run" handicappers who just want to sell a system, get whatever they can, and then run like hell. Good systems, on the other hand, can provide the edge you are looking for, especially if they are educational and not just magic formulae. Such systems are often guaranteed, are developed with considerable effort on the author's part, stress the basics, and, over the long haul, will help you keep your head above water.

PROBATIONARY DRIVER

Chapter 14

Improving Your Chances at the Windows

Professor Kusyshyn and his students have been researching winning factors at the harness races for more than sixteen years. During that time they have looked at over thirty-thousand races and have studied racing programs from most racetracks in North America. Their work has uncovered a number of factors found in the racing program that can be used to increase a handicapper's chances of picking the winner of the race. If you wish to stretch your amusement dollar while at the racetrack, you may want to take these factors into consideration when choosing a horse to wager on. The only prerequisite to using these factors is the ability to know how to read the program. (Please refer to the section in this book on *How To Read The Program* if you have not already done so.)

The research has shown that horses with the factors or characteristics listed win more often than horses not possessing those characteristics:

1. A horse that finished first or second in his last race wins more often.

2. A horse who has a faster speed in his last race than the other horses in today's race wins more often.

3. A horse who has a good post position today will win more often than horses with poorer post positions. On a half-mile track good positions are posts 1 to 4, on a 5/8-mile track good posts are posts 1 to 5, and on one-mile tracks good posts are posts 1 to 6. Your program has the number of wins from each post position at your racetrack. Consult this information for the good posts at your track.

4. A horse who has a good percentage driver on him today will win more often. Driver percentages are usually listed somewhere in your pro-

gram. Consult this list.

5. The horse has won a greater percentage of his races this year than the other horses in the race. In fact, the horse who has won the greatest percentage of races is often a winning wager. That is, he will win often enough at high enough odds for you to show a profit on total investment.

6. The horse improved his position in the last half-mile in his last race. That is, the horse may have come from behind to be first, second or third in the last half-mile. This shows vigor and stamina, and is often an indication that the horse is reaching its physical peak in condition.

7. The horse's last race was within seven days of today's race. Our research has shown that the more recently raced horses win more often.

8. The horse is going off at odds of less than 6 to 1 today. Research by many researchers in the last fifty years has shown that the lower the horse's odds the more often it wins. The favorite, the second favorite, and the third favorite win 60% of all races.

9. The horse's odds today are lower than his odds in his last race. This difference in odds is an indication that the horse is more ready to win today. The horse may be more ready to win today because of a number of factors. Two of the most important are the fact that he is coming back into condition, and he may be racing against easier competition today than he was last week. Professional handicappers pay attention to a horse's warmup as well as his appearance prior to the race. They know the relative classes of the horses that this horse has raced against last week. They take all this information into account when they wager. Thus, we can take advantage of their work and informed opinions by watching the odds board and betting on horses that are going off at lower odds today than they did last week.

10. The horse's last race was on the same racetrack as he's racing on today. In other words, research has shown that local horses win more often than ship-ins. The reason for this is probably because horses that are being shipped in from other tracks are not accustomed to the track surface, to the track's circumference, or to the atmospheric conditions at this particular track. Or they may have had a rough time in the horse trailer en

route. Some horses are very poor shippers and need a couple of weeks to get over their trip.

Professor Kusyshyn can assure you that these factors will greatly increase your chances of coming up with the winner of a race. The way to apply the factors is simply to learn how to read the program and look for these characteristics in each horse in a race. The horse who has more of these properties than the other horses in a race is the most probable winner.

Chapter 15

How to Wager

Wagering language at any track can become confusing to the novice. But with a little explanation and some experience even the novice is able to understand the whole wagering process.

Flat Betting

There are two basic kinds of wagering: *betting flat* and *gimmick wagering*. The least amount that can be wagered is $2.00 on flat bets and $1.00 on gimmicks. Flat betting simply refers to betting a horse to win, place, or show *only* without coupling the horse with another as in the gimmicks (quinella, trifecta, exacta, etc.). When one bets to *win*, then the bettor will only collect a payoff on his pari-mutuel ticket if his horse *wins* the race. If the patron bets a horse to *place*, then he will collect a payoff only if his horse finishes *first* or *second*. It follows, then, that if a person wagers on a horse to *show* he will collect a payoff if his horse comes in *first, second* or *third*.

Normally the payoffs are larger on win tickets rather than place or show. This usually happens because, traditionally, more money is wagered in the win pool and is spread out among the horses. (It is the Win Pool from which the final odds are determined.) Payoffs on place and show tickets normally are less than win tickets due to the fact that more horses share in the payoff. In the Place Pool all the monies bet to place must be distributed to holders of place tickets who wagered to *place* on the eventual winner *or* the horse that came in second.

It should be noted that payoffs always include the wagered money. The payoff on a winning ticket of odds at 3 to 1 would return the holder of that ticket a minimum of $8.00. Consult Figure 15-1 for a better understanding of the odds/payoff ratio for profits of $25.00 or more.

To the novice the process involved in making the wager sometimes appears as complicated as deciding which horse to bet. But raceways are making this task easier to accomplish for all track patrons. While some tracks still use separate windows for betting and cashing, the great majority have changed their pari-mutuel machinery to permit betting and cashing at the same windows. In addition, most raceway past performance programs contain instructions explaining the wagering procedure at their track. Basically, all one has to do is approach the window and inform the seller of the amount one wishes to wager (must be at least $2.00), the number of the horse (as listed in the program), and the position (win, place or show) he elects to wager.

Across the board is a popular term heard around the sellers' windows. This simply refers to a wager covering all three payoff positions. Also known as a *combine,* this ticket (or tickets) actually represents three separate wagers on the same horse in each of the win, place, and show positions. For example, $5.00 across the board on number two means the patron wishes to wager $5.00 to win, $5.00 to place, and $5.00 to show on the number two horse. Such a wager would cost a total of $15.00.

Occasionally, a racetrack will not permit show wagering in a particular race. This occurs in a short field where less than five starters will run the race. Such a decision is allowed by racing commissions across North America to prevent speculators from abusing the minimum $2.10 payoff on any wager. It would be quite easy to wager a considerable sum to show on any of the four horses and still retain a healthy profit at the expense of the track. It follows, then, that in fields where there are less than four starters raceway officials may restrict flat wagering to the win position only.

Gimmick (Feature) Betting

Common feature bets include the daily double, exacta, quinella, and the trifecta. This form of wagering was introduced by raceways to provide variety in betting and to enhance the possibility of the big payoff.

Daily Double: In an attempt to get track patrons to arrive early, racetracks offered the daily double wager as an incentive. A wager on the daily double is a selection which seeks to match the winner in the first race with the winner in the second race. When a bettor's selection in the first race (first half of the double) wins, he is said to be live in the double for the second race. If the bettor's choice in the first race fails to win, then the ticket becomes invalid regardless of which horse wins the second race. The consolation double payoff is an exception. Such an example develops when a scratch or refund occurs in either of the first two races. For example, if a bettor wagered 3-4 in the daily double, and the #3 horse won the first race but the #4 horse was scratched, that patron would be awarded a consolation double payoff. This payoff would be adjusted by track management according to a formula, and it is a significantly smaller amount than the payoff would have been had the #4 horse won the second race.

Since there are a great number of winning combination possibilities, the chances of holding a winning ticket combination are more remote. For instance, if 10 horses were entered in each of the first two races, then there would be 100 different combinations with only one being the eventual winner. Thus, the opportunity for a larger payoff on a $2.00 wager is enhanced. The patron, therefore, is lured to the track early. Some tracks have instituted the late double (picking the winners in the last two races) to entice track patrons to stay to the end of the last race. Gimmick betting also promotes the entertainment and excitement value for race fans. The gimmick wagering pool, however, is separate from the win, place, and show pools. Therefore, even if a favorite wins one of the races, the possibility of a large payoff still exists.

Quinella: In order to win, the bettor must select the first two finishes in a race regardless of their order of finish. Thus, the holder of a 5-7 quinella ticket would collect a payoff if the race finished 5-7 or 7-5.

Exacta (also known as exactor, perfecta): In order to win, the bettor must select the first two finishers in a race *in their exact order of finish*. Thus, the holder of a 2-6 exacta ticket would collect a payoff if the race finished 2-6 but not if #6 won and #2 was second.

Trifecta (also known as triactor): In order to win, the bettor must select the *first three* finishers in a race *in their exact order of finish*. Thus, the holder of a 3-7-1 would only collect a payoff if the #3 horse won, #7 was second, and #1 was third.

Other Variations: The four features discussed comprise the most common gimmick bets and have withstood the test of time. Raceway managements, however, have continued to search for exotic ways of wagering to sustain interest and generate excitement. In recent years other variations have been tried. WIN THREE is a variation of the daily double which seeks to pick the winners in the first three races. In the BIG Q a patron must select the first two finishers in one race, and then exchange these live (winning) tickets for a second winning combination (win and place horse) in another race. POT O GOLD, SUPERFECTA, and BIG FIVE are other variations that have come and gone.

Raceway officials have mixed emotions about exotic wagering. On the one hand, they favor those gimmicks which provide big payoffs and are decided in *one* race; while, on the other hand, they seem to be reluctant to offer more than one occasion (the daily double) where the mutuel pool is frozen awaiting the final outcome in a subsequent race. Track management knows, for example, that track patrons who receive a payoff normally reinvest a significant proportion of their winnings in the next race.

Money Management and the Gimmicks: Depending upon the sophistication of the pari-mutuel equipment at your raceway, a variety of wagering methods are available when playing the gimmicks. The minimum wager remains at $2.00 in these wagering variations.

Reversing the Exacta: Also known as *boxing the exacta,* this variation is commonly used when one has selected two contenders only, with either given an equal chance to win. The patron simply asks the seller for a box ticket on the two horses. For example, a 4-5 box includes the 4-5 and 5-4 combinations and would cost $4.00.

At raceways where the $1.00 box or *part wheel* ticket purchase is permitted, the preceding example would only cost $2.00. In effect, one is only purchasing half tickets; therefore, if one of the combinations wins then the holder of that ticket would receive only half of the winning payoff.

Sometimes the patron has selected three contenders, each of which he believes has an opportunity to win. In this case, a 3-4-6 box would cost $12.00. Such a combination would include the following exacta pairings: 3-4, 4-3, 3-6, 6-3, 4-6, 6-4. Similarly, if the raceway equipment offered $1.00 tickets, then the three horse box just described would cost only $6.00.

It should be noted that when there is an entry in the race, two horses from the same stable, owned by the same owner, then a *separate exacta ticket* must be purchased to cover the possibility that the entry might run 1-2 in the exacta. This situation is *not* covered when one purchases a box ticket. For example, if 1a and 1b constitute an entry, then a patron must purchase a 1-1 ticket separately to cover that possibility.

Exacta/Box/Wagering:

	(Half-ticket)					(Exacta Price)
	$ 1	$ 2	$ 3	$ 4	$ 5	$ 10
2 Horse Box Costs:	$ 2	$ 4	$ 6	$ 8	$ 10	$ 20
3 Horse Box Costs:	$ 6	$12	$18	$24	$ 30	$ 60
4 Horse Box Costs:	$12	$24	$36	$48	$ 60	$120
5 Horse Box Costs:	$20	$40	$60	$80	$100	$200

Boxing the Trifecta: Since the *trifecta* affords a patron the chance at a big payoff he may wish to box his three choices. A 4-1-5 *trifecta box*, for example, costs $12.00 and covers the following trifecta possibilities: 1-4-5, 1-5-4, 4-1-5, 4-5-1, 5-4-1, and 5-1-4. At raceways which permit the $6.00 or half ticket, the 4-1-5 box just illustrated would cost a total $6.00. Trifecta box tickets can be purchased in dollar multiples and matched with three or more horses.

Trifecta/Box/Wagering:

	$ 1	$ 2	$ 3	$ 4	$ 5	$10
3 Horse Box Costs:	$ 6	$ 12	$ 18	$ 24	$ 30	$ 60
4 Horse Box Costs:	$ 12	$ 24	$ 36	$ 48	$ 60	$ 120
5 Horse Box Costs:	$ 60	$ 120	$ 180	$ 240	$ 300	$ 600
6 Horse Box Costs:	$120	$ 240	$ 360	$ 480	$ 600	$1200
7 Horse Box Costs:	$210	$ 420	$ 630	$ 840	$1050	$2100
8 Horse Box Costs:	$336	$ 672	$1008	$1344	$1680	$3360
9 Horse Box Costs:	$504	$1440	$2160	$2880	$3600	$7200

The Key Trifecta Box: Most of the modern machines at raceways today can accommodate the *key box* wagering situation. A patron will use this variation when he has selected a key horse to win the race. The key box permits him to wager his key on top (in the *win* position only) and to box his other contenders for *second* and *third*. If a patron selected #6 as his key and wished to box three other contenders (#7, #8, #9) for second and third, then a key box ticket (at a $1.00 wager) would cost $6.00. The patron would simply step up to the window and ask the mutuel clerk for a $1.00 key trifecta box on #6, with #7, #8 and #9. The 6-7,8,9 *key box* would include the following trifecta possibilities: 6-7-8, 6-7-9, 6-8-7,

6-9-7, 6-8-9, 6-9-8. Please note that the key horse (#6) must win for one of these trifectas to be a winning ticket.

As with trifecta box tickets, the key trifecta box tickets can be purchased in multiples of $1.00. A ($1.00) Key Box with two horses costs $2.00 (two tickets); 6-2-3 = 6-2-3 and 6-3-2 (half tickets only). A ($2.00) Key Box with two horses costs $4.00 (two tickets).

Gimmick: Wheel, Part Wheel and Key Wheel

The *wheel* is a wagering term which refers to wagering a key horse in a gimmick with all the horses. A *front wheel* in the exacta uses the key horse for *first* and all the other horses for *second*. In a 9-horse field, a 7-ALL = 7-1, 7-2, 7-3, 7-4, 7-5, 7-6, 7-8 and 7-9 (8 tickets). Such a wheel ticket can be purchased in multiples of $1.00. Thus, at a $1.00 wager, the previous example would cost $8.00. But if one of those exactas was a winner, then the patron holding the winning ticket would only collect half the winning payoff because he purchased $1.00 tickets.

Sometimes a track patron may wish to wheel his key horse for *second* in the exacta. This is known as a *back wheel*. For example, an ALL-7 exacta (in a 9-horse field) would include the following pairings: 1-7, 2-7, 3-7, 4-7, 5-7, 6-7, 8-7, and 9-7 (8 tickets).

The terms front and back wheel most commonly are used when wagering on the daily double. The front wheel in the daily double asks the patron to select a key horse in the *first race* and then to play it with *all* the horses in the *second race*. In 9-horse fields, a 6-ALL means the patron wishes a 6-1, 6-2, 6-3, 6-4, 6-5, 6-6, 6-7, 6-8, 6-9 (9 tickets). Similarly, if the patron wishes to back wheel a horse he means to wheel all the horses in the *first race* with a *key* horse in the *second race*. An ALL-4 equals 1-4, 2-4, 3-4, 4-4, 5-4, 6-4, 7-4, 8-4, 9-4 (9 tickets).

A *key wheel* in the trifecta is exactly the same as a key trifecta box. That is, a key horse is picked for *first* with *all* the other horses picked for *second* and *third*. In a 9-horse field, for example, a patron may ask the seller for a 6-ALL-ALL which denotes 56 different tickets.

Many patrons prefer not to wheel all the horses in the gimmicks. Some use a *part wheel* in the gimmicks, a wagering luxury which limits the wager only to the contenders, thereby saving wagering capital in the process. Let's take an example to illustrate. The patron selects the #6 as his *key* in the exacta, but only wishes to match it with the 1, 4, and 7 horses. Then he would approach the window and ask for a $1.00 *part wheel—six with the one, four, and seven.* Such a purchase includes 6-1, 6-4, and 6-7 and would cost $3.00 (all half tickets).

The *part wheel,* however, is utilized to advantage in the trifecta and is especially effective when applying the $1.00 wager. It enables the patron to purchase more tickets at a lower cash outlay.

As one example, the track patron eliminates all but five of the horses, but identifies two of them as probable winners. If he figures neither of them will be worse than second, he can set up his part wheel in the following manner. Assuming that #1 and #2 are his probable winners he can ask for $1.00 *part wheel,* 1 *with* the 2 *with the* 3, 4, 5 and 2 *with the* 1 *with the* 3,4,5. Such a purchase costs only $6.00 and includes 6 tickets.

The Post Position Rundown: Perfecta technique was introduced in the first edition of *Stanley's Law* and has gained considerable popularity since that time. It keeps the following two principles in mind: that the inside post positions are a documented advantage in harness racing; and that, while it is difficult enough to handicap for *win,* one should select the inside post positions for *second,* and take *all* the horses for *third.*

Another popular trifecta wager, *two strong contenders,* was introduced in *Stanley's Law.* This situation occurs when the patron has two outstanding contenders (#4 and #7) which he assumes will be part of the trifecta. Again, using the $1.00 wager in a 10-horse field, he asks the seller for 4-7-ALL, 4-ALL-7, 7-4-ALL and 7-ALL-4.

If the patron is concerned that one of the other horses might sneak in for first, he may wish to purchase additional ALL-4-7 and ALL-7-4 tickets.

Gimmicks: A Final Note

It should be noted that with the advances in engineering technology and its application to pari-mutuel equipment, the harness racing patron's wagering techniques are only limited by his imagination. The basic single wager is $2.00, but be alert that some gimmick tickets may have a base price of $3.00. If this occurs, then the $1.00 wager in the box or wheel situation would only return ⅓ of the payoff for each winning $1.00 ticket.

The wagering variations discussed in this section may seem excessive for the novice. But they have been included to give you some idea of how the track regular plays the gimmicks. Such a person attacks the gimmicks buying several tickets without a substantial monetary outlay. And the $1.00 ticket affords him that luxury.

Figure 15-1: Odds/Wagering/Payoff Model

ODDS	TO WIN $25	$50	$75	$100	$150	$200
1-5	$125	$250	$375	$500	$750	$1000
2-5	62.00	125	188	250	375	500
1-2	50	100	150	200	300	400
3-5	42	84	126	168	252	336
4-5	32	64	96	128	192	256
1	26	52	78	104	156	208
6-5	21	42	63	84	126	168
7-5	18	36	54	72	108	144
3-2	17	34	51	68	102	136
8-5	16	32	48	64	96	128
9-5	14	28	42	56	84	112
2	13	25	38	50	75	100
5-2	10	20	30	40	60	80
3	8	16	24	32	48	64
7-2	7	14	21	28	42	56
4	6	12	18	24	36	48
9-2	6	12	17	22	34	44
5	5	10	15	20	30	40
6	4	8	12	16	24	32
7	4	8	10	14	22	28
8	4	6	9	14	20	26
9	4	6	8	12	18	24
10	4	6	8	10	16	20
11	2	4	7	9	14	18
12	2	4	6	9	12	17
13	2	4	6	8	12	16
14	2	4	6	7	11	15
15	2	4	5	7	10	14
16	2	4	5	7	10	13
17	2	4	5	6	8	12
18	2	4	4	6	8	12
19	2	4	4	6	8	11
20	2	4	4	5	8	10
21	2	2	4	5	7	10
22	2	2	4	5	7	9
23	2	2	4	5	7	9
24	2	2	4	4	6	9
25	2	2	4	4	6	8

CHALK HORSE

HARNESS TRIVIA QUIZ

(Answers Courtesy of *Trotting and Pacing Guide* 1981, U.S.T.A.)

1. Which driver holds the record for:
   a) most wins in one day at one track?
   b) most wins on one raceway program (single dashes)?
   c) consecutive wins on one raceway program (single dashes)?
   d) most wins by a driver at one meeting?

2. What is the most money ever won by a driver at one racing meeting?

3. Which driver has recorded the most two-minute drives:
   a) on one raceway program?
   b) at one meeting?

4. Which drivers have had the highest recorded U.D.R.S. percentage in a single year:
   a) for 100-199 starts?
   b) for 200-299 starts?
   c) for 300- up starts?

5. Who is the youngest driver to record a two-minute mile?

6. Name the only father-son driving combination to reach top one million dollars in earnings?

7. Who is the first woman to win a track driving title?

8. Name the horse that has won:
   a) the most heats or dashes, lifetime?
   b) $2-million in two seasons?

9. Which horse has recorded the:
   a) most two-minute miles, lifetime?
   b) most two-minute miles, one year?
   c) most consecutive two-minute miles?
   d) longest winning streak?
   e) most $100,000 races, one year?

10. Which horse holds the world's record for one mile?

11. On the pari-mutuel side, what is:
    a) the record $2 win payoff?
    b) the record U.S. $2 win payoff?
    c) the record $2 place payoff?
    d) the record $2 show payoff?
    e) the record $2 daily double payoff?

12. What is the record single night handle?

13. What is the record for wagering on a single race?

14. What is the record for single night raceway attendance?

15. Which horse has recorded the fastest time as a free-legged pacer?

16. What three races make up the triple crown for 3-year-old trotters?

17. What three races make up the triple crown for 3-year-old pacers?

    (All records are subject to change.)

ANSWERS TO
HARNESS TRIVIA QUIZ

1. (a) 11 by Clint Hodgins, Dufferin Park, Toronto, Ontario, Nov. 25, 1939
        11 by Joe O'Brien, Truro Raceway, Truro, Nova Scotia, Sept. 16, 1942
   (b) 8 by Herve Filion, Hinsdale Raceway, Hinsdale, N.H., Sept. 10, 1978
   (c) 7 by Augustine Ratchford, Sackville Downs, Halifax, N.S., Feb. 21, 1976
   (d) 269 by William O'Donnell, Saratoga Harness, 1979

2. $2,609,399 by John Campbell, The Meadowlands, 1980

3. (a) 5 by Herve Filio, Brandywine Raceway, Wilmington, Del., Aug. 1, 1970
        5 by John Campbell, The Meadowlands, E. Rutherford, N.J., May 24, 1979
   (b) 134 by John Campbell, The Meadowlands, 1980

4. (a) .696 by Fred Johnson, 1951
   (b) .629 by William Miller, 1949
   (c) .566 by C.J. Osborn, 1979

5. 12 yr. old Alma Sheppard at Lexington, *Dean Hanover* TT 1:58.2

6. William Haughton ($1,718,105) and Peter Haughton ($672,903)
   $3,390,903 in 1978 (The pair achieved this performance again in 1977 and 1979.)

7. Beatrice Farber, Northville Downs in 1973 with a .536 U.D.R.S.

8. (a) 350 *Goldsmith Moud* (1864-1877)
        119 *Lenawee Creed* (1963-1975 - modern day record)
   (b) $2,019,213 by *Niatross* (1979-1980)

9. (a) 64 by *Rambling Willie* (1972-1980)
   (b) 24 by *Niatross* (1980)
   (c) 18 by *Niatross* (1980)
   (d) 41 by *Carty Nagle* (1937-1938)
   (e) 9 by *Niatross* (1980) - Pacer
       6 by *Chiola Hanover* (1979) - Trotter

10. *Niatross* (TT 1:49.1) at the Red Mile, 1980

11. (a) $1,120 by *Pat Kuno* at Laviolette Raceway, Three
        Rivers, Quebec, July 26, 1959
    (b) $1,038.60 by *Dr. Brodie* at Marion, Ohio, June
        17, 1944
    (c) $363.60 by *Daring Rodney* at Washington Park,
        Homewood, Ill., Sept. 6, 1962
    (d) $101.20 by *Surmo Hanover* at The Meadowlands E.
        Rutherford, N.J., July 30, 1980
    (e) $8,505.80 *Pilot Me* and *Shadydale Impact,* Pompano
        Park, Fla., Mar. 4, 1968

12. $4,004,246 at The Meadowlands, E. Rutherford, N.J., July
    18, 1980

13. $634,264 bet on The Meadowlands Pace (M:7/18/80)

14. 54,861 at Roosevelt Raceway, Westbury, N.Y., Aug. 20, 1960

15. 1:52 by *Steady Star*, in a time trial, Lexington, Ky., Oct., 1971

16. The Hambletonian, The Kentucky Futurity, and The Yonkers Trot

17. The Cane Pace, The Little Brown Jug, and The Messenger Stake

Roster of Extended Pari-Mutuel Tracks

(Courtesy of *Trotting & Racing Guide* 1981, U.S.T.A.)

U.S. TRACKS	Track Size	Location
Atlantic City Raceway	(5/8)	Atlantic City, NJ
Audubon Raceway	(1/2)	Henderson, KY
Balmoral Park	(5/8)	Crete, IL
Bangor Raceway	(1/2)	Bangor, ME
Batavia Downs	(1/2)	Batavia, ME
Brandywine Raceway	(5/8)	Wilmington, DE
Buffalo Raceway	(1/2)	Hamburg, NY
Cumberland Raceway	(1/2)	West Cumberland, ME
Dover Downs	(5/8)	Dover, DE
Fairmont Park	(1m)	Collineville, IL
Fox Fields	(1/2)	N. Aurora, IL
Foxboro Raceway	(5/8)	Foxboro, MA
Freehold Raceway	(1/2)	Freehold, NJ
Freestate Raceway	(5/8)	Laurel, MD
Golden Bear Raceway	(1m)	Sacramento, CA
Harrington Raceway	(1/2)	Harrington, DE
Hawthorne	(1m)	Cicero, IL
Hazel Park	(5/8)	Hazel Park, MI
Hinsdale Raceway	(1/2)	Hinsdale, NH
Hollywood Park	(1m)	Inglewood, CA
Jackson Raceway	(1/2)	Jackson, MI
Latonia Raceway	(1m)	Florence, KY
Lebanon Raceway	(1/2)	Lebanon, OH
Lewiston Raceway	(1/2)	Lewiston, ME
Liberty Bell Park	(5/8)	Philadelphia, PA
Los Alamitos Raceway	(5/8)	Los Alamitos, CA
Louisville Downs	(1/2)	Louisville, KY
Maywood Park	(1/2)	Maywood, IL
Monticello Raceway	(1/2)	Monticello, NY
Northfield Park	(1/2)	Northfield, OH
Northville Downs	(1/2)	Northville, MI

Ocean Downs	(1/2)	Berlin, MD
Pocono Downs	(5/8)	Wilkes-Barre, PA
Pompano Park	(5/8)	Pompano Beach, FL
Quad City Downs	(5/8)	East Moline, IL
Raceway Park	(5/8)	Toledo, OH
Rockingham Park	(1/2)	Salem, NH
Roosevelt Raceway	(1/2)	Westbury, NY
Rosecroft Raceway	(1/2)	Oxon Hill, MD
Saginaw Valley Downs	(1/2)	Saginaw, MI
Saratoga Harness	(1/2)	Saratoga, NY
Scarborough Downs	(1/2)	Scarborough, ME
Scioto Downs	(5/8)	Columbus, OH
Sportsman's Park	(5/8)	Cicero, IL
The Meadows	(5/8)	Meadow Lands, PA
The Red Mile	(1m)	E. Rutherford, NJ
Vernon Downs	(3/4)	Vernon, NY
Wolverine Raceway	(1m)	Livonia, MI
Yonkers Raceway	(1/2)	Yonkers, NY

Canadian Tracks

Barrie Raceway	(1/2)	Barrie, Ontario
Blue Bonnets Raceway	(5/8)	Montreal, Quebec
Brunswick Downs	(1/2)	Dieppe, New Brunswick
Cloverdale Raceway	(1/2)	Surrey, British Columbia
Connaught Park	(1/2)	Lucerne, Quebec
Dresden Raceway	(1/2)	Dresden, Ontario
Elmira Raceway	(1/2)	Elmira, Ontario
Flamboro Downs	(1/2)	Dundas, Ontario
Greenwood Raceway	(5/8)	Toronto, Ontario
Kawartha Downs	(5/8)	Fraserville, Ontario
Kingston Park Raceway	(5/8)	Kingston, Ontario
Marquis Downs	(5/8)	Saskatoon, Alberta
Mohawk Raceway	(5/8)	Rexdale, Ontario
Northlands Park	(5/8)	Edmonton, Alberta
Orangeville Raceway	(1/2)	Orangeville, Ontario
Quebec Hippodrome	(1/2)	Quebec City, Quebec
Regina Raceway	(1/2)	Regina, Saskatchewan
Rideau Carleton Raceway	(5/8)	Ottawa, Ontario
Sackville Downs	(1/2)	Lower Sackville, Nova Scotia

Sandown Park	(5/8)	Sidney, British Columbia
Stampede Park	(5/8)	Calgary, Alberta
Sudbury Downs	(1/2)	Chelmsford, Ontario
Western Fair Raceway	(1/2)	London, Ontario
Windsor Raceway	(5/8)	Windsor, Ontario

About the Authors

Dr. Kusyshyn is a university professor of gambling, an author, and gambler. He has authored five books on gambling including *The World's Greatest Blackjack Book* (with Dr. Carl Cooper), *Harness Racing Gold,* and *Blackjack Gold.* He has also developed, with the aid of a computer, winning systems for blackjack, hockey, football and racing. His students have won millions of dollars with his systems. Each of his systems carries a guarantee to show a profit on any statistically fair sample of events.

Dr. Kusyshyn and his students have conducted and published research studies on the psychology of professional and social gamblers. They have developed a new theory of human motivation on the basis of their research findings.

Dr. Kusyshyn has appeared on many radio and TV talk shows. He is recognized as the world's academic authority on gambling and is a member of many professional associations including the New York Academy of Sciences, the British Society for the Study of Gambling, the U.S. and Canadian Trotting Associations, and the American and Canadian Psychological Associations. He is listed in the Directory of American Men and Women of Science.

Al Stanley has been a successful part-time professional handicapper on the Windsor-Detroit area harness circuit for the past ten years. He works for one of the Big Three auto-makers by day and faithfully attends the standardbreds at night. Hungry to become a successful turf speculator, this high school dropout has devoured all of the available literature about handicapping the standardbreds and about the sport in general. People around the track have observed the thoroughness of this accomplished handicapper and have come to recognize Al Stanley as a learned authority on everything connected with the harness racing industry. When a group of local people decided to form a harness racing stable they sought out Al for his expertise and gladly welcomed him as a full partner into their new corporation.

Sam Dragich is an elementary school principal with a Master of Education degree in educational administration. As an educational consultant for Ecolad Corporation he has successfully designed the Ricky Receptacle Litter Control Program for primary school children. For the past six years he has served prominently on the Advisory Board to TV Ontario, the province's educational television network.

Five years ago Sam Dragich began to attend the harness races quite regularly. Like most people at the track he tore up abundantly more tickets than he cashed. So when the opportunity came to become a partner in a racing stable he jumped at the chance of being *on the inside*. But he learned—and not too quickly at that—that horsemen usually overestimate their own horse's chances of winning. He continued to be a loser until he teamed up with Al Stanley.

While *The Gambling Times Guide To Harness Racing* provides a comprehensive introduction to the sport and business of harness racing, the authors' two other books focus on handicapping and winning at the races. These books present two complementary approaches to winning. Professor Kusyshyn's book, *Harness Racing Gold*, concentrates on scientifically-based information gathered over thousands of races and presents the Simple Point Method for unearthing winners. *Stanley's Law,* a 136-page textbook, focuses on pre-race warm-ups, current form, class, and bargain prices. The author provides new insights into playing the gimmicks—a notable feature for those fans looking for the big score.

If *The Gambling Times Guide To Harness Racing* has kindled a curiosity about winning at the harness races, we recommend *Harness Racing Gold* and *Stanley's Law* to you. Both texts are easy to read and understand, reasonably priced, and carry an unconditional guarantee and refund privileges.

GLOSSARY OF TERMS

Across the Board: Wagering term which refers to betting a horse to *win*, to *place* and to *show*.

Action: A horse gets "action" when it gets a noticeable increase in public money on the tote board causing its odds to drop.

Added Money Event: Race in which nomination and entrance fees are added to the purse.

Age: A horse's age is reckoned from January 1 of the year of foaling. Horses eligible to race at extended parimutuel meetings must be at least *two* and not more than *fourteen* years of age.

All Out: Expression which refers to a horse having given his all during a race and having no energy left for another brush.

Also Eligible: (AE) Horse which meets the eligibility conditions for the race and will draw in if a horse is scratched.

Angle: Handicapping term which may be a factor in determining the outcome of a race.

Auctions: Annual sales of race horses and yearlings.

Back-Wheel: Wagering term used in feature or gimmick races which refers to wheeling a *key* horse for *second*. When used in the Daily Double it refers to matching all the horses in the first race with a key horse in the second race.

Back-Up Bet: Wagering term which refers to protecting an original wager. Also known as a saver, this may refer to betting a horse to *place, reversing an exacta, boxing a trifecta,* etc.

Bad Actor: Horse which is difficult for the driver to control. Also known as a *hothead*.

Barn Money: Substantial sum in the mutuel pools attributed to insiders rather than the public. Also known as *smart money*.

Beaten Favorite: Handicapping term noting horse was loser in a race where he was the favorite.

Bet Down:	Wagering term referring to a horse whose odds are decreasing as more money is wagered on it.
Bike:	Sulky used for racing or training.
Bike Change:	Handicapping term indicating that the horse changed from a conventional to a modified bike, or vice versa.
Blindswitch:	Racing term which refers to horse getting boxed in through an action of his driver.
Blowout:	Final (fairly fast) workout of a horse a day before it races.
Box:	Wagering term used in the gimmicks to match all of the numbers you wish with each other.
Boxed In:	Horse is unable to pull out from the rail as he is trapped in on all sides by the other horses.
Brace Bandages:	Stretch bandages wrapped around a horse's legs to protect him from hitting his legs. Also worn to make a horse's legs stronger when he is lame.
Break:	When a horse goes off his gait (trot or pace). A horse that breaks stride in a race must move to the outside, slow down and try to regain his stride.
Breakage:	Money which the track keeps after the mutuel pool has been equally distributed (to the nearest dime) to patrons holding winning tickets.
Broodmare:	Mare which has retired from racing for breeding purposes.
Brush:	Burst of speed (high expenditure of energy) over a short distance (usually for 1/16 of a mile). Also known as a *move*.
Call:	Each of the listed poles or positions in a racing line in the program including the *start, finish* and the ¼, ½ and ¾ poles. Also known as a *pole*.
Catch Driver:	One who is hired or assigned to drive on race day to replace the original or yet-to-be announced driver.
Chalk:	The race favorite.
Chalk Player:	Track patron who always wagers on the favorite.
Challenge:	Race beside the leader in an attempt to overtake him.

BOXED IN

Check Rein:	A harness line or strip used to keep the horse's head high.
Claiming Race:	A race in which any horseman may purchase (claim) an entered horse for the amount specified at time of entry.
Choked Down:	Horse that had difficulty breathing during a race.
Class:	Refers to classification rating of horses.
Clocker:	Handicapper who times the main workouts of horses one hour before their call to post.
Clocking:	The fractions timed in the main warmup (see Clocker).
Close:	Having the ability and stamina for a final rush to the finish line.
Closer:	Horse that consistently comes from behind in a race.
Condition:	A term set down in a conditioned race. A horse is said to be in condition when he is ready to exert a superb winning effort. Also known as *shape* or *sharpness*.
Colt:	A male horse under four years of age.
Conditioned Race:	Race in which eligibility is determined according to specified qualifications (earnings, age, sex, finish position in previous races, etc.).
Condition Line:	A racing line in a past performance program which shows that a horse is ready to exert a superb winning effort.
Contender:	A horse considered to have a good chance of winning a race by a handicapper.
Conventional Bike:	Known as the old racing bike, it has been replaced at larger tracks by the modified bike.
Cover:	Horse and driver get cover when they race behind another horse which acts as a windbreak for them. Such an action uses up less of the horse's energy.
Cracking Down:	Out to win today.
C.T.A.:	Canadian Trotting Association, major governing body of harness racing in Canada. Publish *Trot* magazine (harness racing monthly).
Curve:	See *Turn*.

Daily Double:	A feature wager matching the winner in the first race with the winner in the second.
Dam:	Mare which gave birth to a race horse. Usually listed second (after the sire) in a past performance program.
Dead Heat:	Two or more horses finishing exactly even.
Disqualification:	When a horse is placed last due to a racing infraction, regardless of its original finish.
Distanced:	Horse finishing more than 25 lengths behind winner.
Double Gaited:	Horse that can both trot and pace.
Dropping Down:	Handicapping term which refers to a horse entered in a class lower than his previous race.
Early Money:	Reference to a horse getting lots of action (substantial sum of money) on the tote board as soon as the windows open for a race.
Elimination Heat:	Heats of a race split to qualify the horses for the final heat. Purse money normally progresses higher with successive heats.
Exacta Pool:	Refers to the total monies that have been wagered on the exacta on a race.
Engine, on the:	Horse out in front; leading.
Entry:	Two or more horses having a common interest (same owner, trainer, etc.).
Exacta:	Gimmick wagering term which refers to selecting the first two horses in a race in the exact order of finish.
False Favorite:	Horse which the public has overbet that loses.
Favorite:	Horse in a race on which the public wagers the most money (goes off at the lowest odds). Wins about 33% of the time.
Feature:	Any race in which the mutuel payoff is won by combining two or more horses (daily double, exacta, quinella, trifecta, etc.). Also known as a *gimmick*.
Field, the:	Occurs in races with more horses than the number of post positions listed on the tote board. Those extra horses can be bet together as the field using the last post position number

	when calling your wager.
Field, Full:	When there are the same number of horses entered in a race as there are post positions listed on the tote board.
Filly:	A female horse under four years of age.
Flat Bet:	Wagering to *win, place* or *show* (not a gimmick bet).
Flush Out:	A driving tactic whereby a trailing driver looking for cover entices a horse in front of him to leave the rail.
Follow:	Young horses are taught to follow or stay behind another horse until called upon to pull out.
Fraction:	Refers to the lapsed time to the nearest 1/5 of a second at the 1/4, 1/2, 3/4 and mile calls in a race.
Free-for-All:	Race for the best horses (according to money earned or quality of races won).
Free-legged:	Term that refers to a pacer which races without hopples.
Front Runner:	Horse that likes to race in front leading the others.
Front Wheel:	Gimmick term which refers to matching a *key* horse for *first* with all the other horses for *second*. In a daily double it refers to matching a *key* horse in the first race with all the horses in the second.
Futurity:	A stake in which the dam of the competing animal, or the animal itself, is nominated either when in foal or during the year of foaling.
Gait:	Required trotting or pacing stride.
Gelding:	A neutered male horse.
Gimmick:	See *Feature.*
Green Horse:	Never raced or only raced a few times.
Half-ticket:	Refers to a $1.00 wager on a feature combination. Such a winning ticket is entitled to half the winning payoff.
Handicap:	Speculation on the outcome of a race identifying contenders and non-contenders and ultimately making a selection to wager.
Handicap Race:	Race in which post positions are assigned according to class.

Handle:	Refers to the total monies wagered in all the pools on a single racing card.
Head Pole:	A billiard cue used to keep a horse's head straight.
Head-to-Head:	Two horses that are challenging each other down the stretch or racing side by side during a race.
Heat:	See *Elimination Heat.*
Hopples:	Leather straps worn around a pacer's legs to keep him on gait. The straps are connected to the front and rear legs so that each side can move separately.
Horse:	Male horse 4 years of age or older.
Horseman:	An owner, driver, trainer, or groom of a racehorse.
Hothead:	See *Bad Actor.*
H.T.A.:	Harness Tracks of America.
Impeded:	Occurs in a race where the horse is prevented from moving forward, thus losing ground.
Inquiry:	When the judges investigate a race to see if any infractions of the rules took place.
Inside (Post):	One of the post positions closer to the rail (an advantage in harness racing).
Interference:	Occurs when a driver commits an "illegal" act (even if accidental) which denies another horse fair access to any part of the track.
Interference Break:	Occurs when a horse breaks stride because of the action of another horse or driver.
In the money:	Finishing *first, second,* or *third* allowing winning ticket holders a mutuel payoff.
Invitational:	Race for the best horses both on and off the grounds. The racing secretary normally issues an invitation and offers a suitable purse.
Jog Cart:	Also known as a *training bike.* It is longer and heavier than a racing bike; mainly used for training, the jog cart is unsuitable for racing.
Jogged:	Term used to describe a horse winning a race with ease.
Judges:	Individuals who determine official results at the end of a race and enforce the rules of racing.
Key (horse):	Selection of a horse to be included in all gimmick

purchases.

Lapped On Break: Occurs at the finish when any part of a horse is alongside the hindquarters of the horse ahead which is breaking.

Late Money: Reference to a horse getting lots of action (substantial sum of money) on the tote board just before the mutuel windows close for a race.

Leaves: Term refers to a horse that gives a burst of speed at the start of a race to gain a good position on the rail.

Lengths Behind: A statistic found in a past performance program which gives a horse's lengths behind the leader, normally at the 1/2, 3/4, stretch and mile calls in a race.

Live: A horse is said to be *live* when it shows it is out to win.

Live (in double): When patron says he's *live in the double* it means he is holding some daily double tickets that are matched with the first race winner.

Lock: Term refers to a horse that has everything going for him (good post, best driver, action on the tote board, class of race, etc.). Also known as a *standout*.

Locked In: See *Boxed In*.

Longshot: Horse given little chance (high odds) of winning the race. If it does win it will give a bigger payoff.

Maiden: Any horse that has not won a pari-mutuel race.

Mare: Female horse four years of age or older.

Modified Bike: Approved racing bike presently in use at most tracks.

Morning Line: The track handicapper's prediction (as printed in the program) of what the final odds of each horse will be at post time.

Move: Any effort to improve a horse's position during a race. See *Brush*.

Moving Up: Handicapping term which refers to a horse entered in a class higher than that of his previous race.

Mudder: Handicapping term which refers to a horse's ability to race as well on an off track as it can on

	one that is fast.
Mutuel:	The payoff on a $2.00 ticket.
Non-Winners (NW):	Classification used by racing secretary. (NW 600 L5 means horses may be entered in this conditioned race if they had not earned $600 in their last 5 starts.)
Objection:	Indication on tote board that a driver has lodged a complaint against another driver.
Odds:	The chances a horse has of winning.
Off:	Track is said to be *off* when the racing surface is other than fast (muddy, sloppy, slow, etc.).
On his oats:	Horse is racing without benefit of stimulants.
On the wood:	Term used to describe a horse that is racing along the rail.
On top:	Term used to describe a horse that is leading.
Outside (post):	Refers to a horse racing farthest from the rail.
Overlay:	Horse whose chances of winning are greater than the odds the public has given it.
Pacer:	Horse that races with hopples and whose strides conform to the pacing gait (the legs on the left side move in unison, then the right side, and so on. A laterally gaited horse).
Paddock:	A restricted area near the racing surface where horses are detained just before racing. *Paddocking* a horse refers to all the preparations before and after racing.
Parked Out:	Refers to a horse racing on the outside beside the horses closer to the rail. This uses up considerable energy and increases the distance a horse must travel.
Parlay:	Taking all the money you win on one wager and betting it all on your next wager.
Partial Wheel:	Playing a *key* horse with some (not all) of the other horses.
Past Performance Line:	Racing lines for each horse printed in the track's program showing that horse's position at every call in each of his previous (usually 5 or 6) races.
Payoff:	The return on a winning mutuel ticket.
Perfecta:	See *Exacta*.

Perfect Trip:	Horse that sits on the rail behind the leader until the stretch and then shoots to the front to win is said to have had a *perfect trip*.
Photo Finish:	A photograph taken at the finish line to help the judges decide the official results.
Place:	Finish *second*.
Place Pool:	Refers to the total monies that have been wagered in the *place* position on all the horses in a race.
Play:	Wager.
Pole:	Same as *Call*.
Post Parade:	The formal announcing of the horses about 8 minutes prior to post. Horses are often led by a parade marshall on horseback before the public in the stands.
Preferred:	Classification for the better horses, just a notch below Open Invitational and Free-for-All.
Price:	See *Payoff*.
Provisional Driver:	One who has not yet completed the satisfactory number of successful drives to qualify for his official Driver's License.
Puller:	Horse that is always straining to go. Not a good sign as such horses usually take the lead for most of the race, then run out of gas well before they get to the finish line.
Pulled Out:	Horse that moved from the rail to the outside to improve its position.
Purse:	Money that is awarded to the owners of the horses finishing in the first five positions. Normal distribution is as follows: *first,* 50% of purse; *second,* 25%; *third,* 12%; *fourth,* 8%; *fifth* 5%.
Qualifier:	A non-betting race in which horses must meet a certain time standard to qualify for entry into a pari-mutuel race. Horses that are laid off a long time, that have made a break in consecutive races, or were greatly outdistanced in their last race could be made to qualify by the race secretary.
Racing Line:	See *Past Performance Line*.

Rail:	The inside railing around a track.
Rail Opens:	Occurs near the finish when the leading horse tires and veers to the right allowing the horse trailing to pass on the inside.
Recall:	Starter's decision to restart the race. Usually occurs near the starting pole when the starter sees that not all the horses will get a fair start.
Record:	The horse's lifetime mark is achieved when he records his fastest winning time in any race against time (includes time trial, qualifier, and pari-mutuel racing).
Recovered:	Refers to a horse that has regained his gait after encountering difficulty in the early going.
Result Charts:	Compiled by a track official, gives a statistical description in each race of every horse's position at each call. The result charts contain the official results information (fractions, final time, mutuel payoffs, horse being claimed, etc.).
Reverse:	Refers to boxing an exacta combination.
Roughgaited:	Horse that temporarily goes off stride. The horse either recovers from this difficulty or breaks stride.
Rundown:	Wagering term which refers to matching a horse in the gimmicks with several or all of the other horses.
Scratch:	Removal of a horse from a race (usually done by the track veterinarian due to the horse becoming ill or injured).
Selection:	The horse (or gimmick combination) you have finally decided to wager upon.
Set Down:	A driver is *set down* (suspended) by the judges when he has violated a racing rule.
Shape:	See *Condition*.
Sharp:	See *Condition*.
Ship In:	Horse racing at a track for the first time after being shipped-in from another track.
Short:	Horse is said to come up short when it seemingly runs out of gas a short distance before the finish.
Show:	A *third* place finish.
Show Pool:	Refers to the total monies that have been

wagered in the *show* position on all the horses in the race.

Shuffled Back: Reference to a horse that is prevented from moving forward (usually just after the start) by the horse(s) in front. Such action causes the horse to lose ground and take a less desirable position in the pack.

Shut Out: Arrival to wager after the mutuel window has closed.

Sire: Father of a race horse. A horse's sire is always listed first where the birth information is printed in the past performance program.

Smart Money: See *Barn Money*.

Spreader(s): A piece of rubber or vinyl hose which is looped around a horse's upper front leg(s). It spreads the horse's legs apart sufficiently to prevent the horse from hitting his knees during a race.

Stake(s): Race in which the purse is made up by contributions from the track, the government, and in entry fees. Have become increasingly lucrative and popular in recent years in the form of sires stakes races.

Stallion: Male horse used for stud (breeding purposes). Such horses normally retire from racing to service mares, generally for a fee.

Standardbred: Term which usually identifies a harness racehorse — trotter or pacer.

Standout: Handicapping term identifying a horse that appears to have everything positive going for it when compared to the other horses.

Steward: A racing official.

Stiff: Term refers to a driver holding a horse back (which is illegal and punishable by fine and/or suspension).

Stretch: Straightaway on a track. Usually refers to the last 1/8-mile of a race.

Sulky: See *Bike*.

Sure Thing: Horse will win for sure (mythical phrase as anything can happen in a horse race to upset the odds).

Switches: Phrase refers to a patron changing from one handicapping method to another, and then having a horse win by the former method.

System: Handicapping method which dictates a systematic form of play and win.

Take: Refers to that portion of the mutuel handle (approx. 17%) to which the track and government is entitled.

Ticket: A pari-mutuel wager in ticket form.

Tightener: When a horse comes up after a layoff, it can be said that such a race is a *tightener* for his next race. Hopefully the horse will be stronger for his next appearance.

Time Trial: Race against time where official clock is used and where other horses (including thoroughbreds) may be used to encourage the horse to greater speed.

Tote Board: Short for the totalisator board which normally is situated in the infield and flashes up-to-the-minute wagering information (approximate odds, win, place, and show-pools, minutes to post, gimmick payoffs, etc.).

Tout: One who gives or sells information regarding the outcome or races.

Trailer: Horse that starts in the second tier (behind the first line of horses). This occurs when the number of horses starting exceeds the number of starting places on the mobile starting gate.

Trailing: Horse in advantageous position directly behind the leader.

Train: Working out with a horse simulating parts of a race.

Trainer: Licensed horseman who gets a horse ready to race. Traditionally, he gets 5% of any purse money the horse wins.

Training Mile: A fast workout simulating all parts of a race.

Trifecta: Gimmick wagering term which selects the first three finishers of a race in their exact order of

WHEELING A HORSE

	finish. Also known as *triactor*.
Trifecta Pool:	Refers to the total monies that have been wagered on the trifecta in a race.
Trot:	The opposite legs move at the same time. Race with a high-stepping gait.
Tucked:	Term that describes a horse settling in on the rail after leaving or being parked out.
Turn:	A curve around a racing surface. Horses at a mile track make 2 *turns,* at a 5/8-mile track make 3 *turns,* and at a 1/2-mile track make 4 *turns.*
U.D.R.S.:	Universal Driver Rating System is to harness racing as the batting average is to baseball.
Uncovered:	Also known as *without cover* or *having no cover,* this expression refers to a horse that has left the security of racing behind another horse.
Underlay:	Handicapping term refers to a horse whose chances of winning are less than the odds the public has given it.
U.S.T.A.:	United States Trotting Association, the major governing body of harness racing in the United States. Publish monthly harness racing magazine, *Hoof Beats.*
Variance:	Rating system which seeks to equalize mile speeds at different tracks.
Wager:	Play or bet.
Wagering Unit:	When adopting a systematic method of play it refers to wagering the same amount on every play.
Warmup:	Refers to the jogging activity on race night. The main warmup occurs one hour before post time when the trainer goes a warmup mile (at a lesser speed) simulating what he wants the horse to do during the race. Also known as a *working out.*
Well-gaited:	Refers to a horse that is exhibiting perfect stride (trot or pace).
Wheel:	Matching a key horse with all the other horses in any gimmick wagering situation.
Win:	Finishing first.
Winner:	The horse whose nose is the first to touch the finish wire.

Winners Over:	Classification term used by the racing secretary (WO5000 81 means such a conditioned race is open to horses that have won over $5000 in 1981.)
Wire:	The finish line (imaginary). However, there is a finish wire suspended above the track which is in line with the photo finish camera.
Workout:	See *Warmup.*
Workout (for judges):	Instead of being asked to run in a qualifying race, a better horse may be granted an official workout for judges instead.
Yearling:	Horse between 1 and 2 years of age (thus, ineligible for racing.)

KEEPING YOUR GAMING
KNOWLEDGE CURRENT

Expert horse race handicappers Mark Cramer, Harvey Green-field and Barry Meadow all write monthly columns for *Gambling Times* magazine, and horse racing is regularly the subject of feature articles. Now that you've read *The Gambling Times Guide To Harness Racing*, and know more about how to tackle harness handicapping, it's important to keep abreast of the rapid and continuous changes and developments in this area. The best way to do that is with a subscription to *Gambling Times* magazine.

Since February of 1977, readers of *Gambling Times* magazine have profited immensely. They have done so by using the information they have read each month. If that sounds like a simple solution to winning more and losing less, well it is! Readers look to *Gambling Times* for that very specific reason. And it delivers.

Gambling Times is totally dedicated to showing readers how to win more money in every form of legalized gambling. How much you're going to win depends on many factors, but it's going to be considerably more than the cost of a subscription.

WINNING AND MONEY

Winning, that's what *Gambling Times* is all about. And money, that's what *Gambling Times* is all about. Because winning and money go hand in hand.

Here's what the late Vince Lombardi, the famous football coach of the Green Bay Packers, had to say about winning:

"It's not a sometime thing. Winning is a habit. There is no room for second place. There is only one place in my game and that is first place. I have finished second twice in my time at Green Bay and I don't ever want to finish second again. The objective is to win—fairly, squarely, decently, by the rules—but to win. To beat the other guy. Maybe that sounds hard or cruel. I don't think it is. It is and has always been an American zeal to be first in anything we do, and to win, and to win and to win."

Mr. Lombardi firmly believed that being a winner is "man's finest hour." *Gambling Times* believes it is too, while being a loser is depressing, ego-deflating, expensive and usually very lonely. "Everybody loves a winner" may be a cliche, but it's true. Winners command respect and are greatly admired. Winners are also very popular and have an abundance of friends. You may have seen many a winner in a casino, with a bevy of girls surrounding him . . . or remember one who could get just about any girl he wanted.

Some of the greatest gamblers in the world also have strong views on what winning is all about. Here's what two of them have to say on the subject:

> "To be a winner, a man has to feel good about himself and know he has some kind of advantage going in. I never made bets on even chances. Smart is better than lucky."—"Titanic" Thompson

> "When it comes to winnin', I got me a one-track mind. You gotta want to win more than anything else. And you gotta have confidence. You can't pretend to have it. That's no good. You gotta have it. You gotta know. Guessers are losers. Gamblin's just as simple as that."—Johnny Moss

Gambling Times will bring you the knowledge you need to come home a winner and come home in the money. For it is knowledge, the kind of knowledge you'll get in its pages, that separates winners from losers. It's winning and money that *Gambling Times* offers you.

Gambling Times will be your working manual to winning wealth.

The current distribution of this magazine is limited to selected newsstands in selected cities. Additionally, at newsstands where it is available, it's being snapped up, as soon as it's displayed, by gamblers who know a sure bet when they see one.

So if you're serious about winning, you're best off subscribing to *Gambling Times*. Then you can always count on its being there, conveniently delivered to your mailbox—and what's more, it will be there one to two weeks before it appears on the newsstands. You'll be among the first to receive the current issue as soon as it comes off the presses, and being first is the way to be a winner.

Having every monthly issue of *Gambling Times* will enable you to build an "Encyclopedia of Gambling," since the contents of this magazine are full of sound advice that will be as good in five or ten years as it is now.

As you can see, a subscription to *Gambling Times* is your best bet for a future of knowledgeable gambling. It's your ticket to *WINNING* and *MONEY.*

Take the time to read the following offer. As you can see, *Gambling Times* has gone all out to give you outstanding bonuses. You can join the knowledgeable players who have learned that *Gambling Times* helps them to win more money.

FOUR NEW WAYS TO GET 12 WINNING ISSUES OF *GAMBLING TIMES* FREE...

Every month over 250,000 readers trust *Gambling Times* to introduce powerful new winning strategies and systems. Using proven scientific methods, the world's leading experts show you how to win big money in the complex field of gambling.

Gambling Times has shown how progressive slot machines can be beat. Readers have discovered important new edges in blackjack. They've been shown how to know for sure when an opponent is bluffing at poker. *Gambling Times* has also spelled out winning methods for football, baseball and basketball. They've published profound new ways of beating horses. Their team of experts will uncover information in the months ahead that's certain to be worth thousands of dollars to you.

In fact, the features are so revolutionary that they must take special precautions to make sure *Gambling Times* readers learn these secrets long before anyone else. So how much is *Gambling Times* worth to you? Well...

NOW *GAMBLING TIMES* CAN BE BETTER THAN FREE! Here's how: This BONUS package comes AUTOMATICALLY TO YOU WHEN YOU SUBSCRIBE...or goes to a friend if you give a gift subscription.

(1) POKER BONUS at the TROPICANA card room in Las Vegas. Play poker at the TROPICANA and receive a free dinner buffet and comps to the "Folies Bergere" show for you *and* a guest. Value exceeds $40 excluding gratuities.

(2) FREE SPORTS BET. CHURCHILL DOWNS SPORTS BOOK in Las Vegas will let you make one wager up to $300 with no "vigorish." This means instead of laying the usual 11-to-10 odds, you can actually bet even up! You can easily save $30 here.

(3) PAYOFF BIGGER THAN THE TRACK. LEROY'S RACE BOOK, in Las Vegas, will add 10% to your payoff (up to $30 extra) on a special bet. Just pick the horse and the race of your choice, anywhere in America. For the first time in history, you can win more than the track pays.

(4) OUTSTANDING ROOM DISCOUNTS available only to *Gambling Times* subscribers. Check in at the SANDS in Las Vegas or Atlantic City, the TROPICANA in Atlantic City, the HIGH SIERRA in Lake Tahoe, or the CONDADO INN & CASINO in San Juan, Puerto Rico. Stay for 3 days and 2 nights and you'll save $29 off their normal low rates.

THAT'S A SAVING GREATER THAN THE ENTIRE COST OF YOUR SUBSCRIPTION.

USE ALL FOUR CERTIFICATES (VALID FOR ONE YEAR)...GET *GAMBLING TIMES* FREE...AND YOU'LL PUT $93 IN YOUR POCKET!

To begin your delivery of *Gambling Times* magazine at once, enclose a payment of $36.00 by check or money order (U.S. currency), MasterCard or Visa. Add $5.00 per year for postage outside the United States.

GAMBLING TIMES MAGAZINE
1018 N. Cole Avenue
Hollywood, California 90038

GAMBLING TIMES
MONEY BACK GUARANTEE

If at any time you decide *Gambling Times* is not for you, you will receive a full refund on all unmailed copies. You are under no obligation and may keep the bonus as a gift.

Other Valuable Sources of Knowledge Available Through *Gambling Times*

(See ordering information on page 146.)

Here are some additional sources you can turn to for worthwhile gambling information:

The Experts Sports Handicapping Newsletter.

Published monthly, this newsletter will show you how to become an Expert handicapper. You will learn the different styles of handicapping and be able to select the one method best suited to your personality. Yearly subscriptions are $60; $50 for *Gambling Times* subscribers.

The Experts Blackjack Newsletter.

This monthly newsletter has all the top blackjack Experts working just for you. Features answers, strategies and insights that were never before possible. Yearly subscriptions are $60; $50 for *Gambling Times* subscribers.

Poker Player.

Published every other week, this *Gambling Times* newspaper features the best writers and theorists on the poker scene today. You will learn all aspects of poker, from odds to psychology, as well as how to play in no-limit competition and in tournaments. Yearly subscriptions (26 issues) are $20.

OTHER BOOKS AVAILABLE

If you can't find the following books at your local bookstore, they may be ordered directly from *Gambling Times,* 1018 N. Cole Ave., Hollywood, CA 90038. Information on how to order is on page 146.

Poker Books

According to Doyle by Doyle Brunson—Acknowledged by most people as the world's best all-around poker player, twice World Champion Doyle Brunson brings you his homespun wisdom from over 30 years as a professional poker player. This book will not only show you how to win at poker, it will give you valuable insights into how to better handle that poker game called LIFE.
Softbound. $6.95. (ISBN: 0-89746-003-0)

Caro on Gambling by Mike Caro—The world's leading poker writer covers all the aspects of gambling from his regular columns in *Gambling Times* magazine and *Poker Player* newspaper. Discussing odds and probabilities, bluffing and raising, psychology and character, this book will bring to light valuable concepts that can be turned into instant profits in home games as well as in the poker palaces of the West.
Softbound. $6.95. (ISBN: 0-89746-029-4)

Caro's Book of Tells by Mike Caro—The photographic body language of poker. Approximately 150 photographs with text explaining when a player is bluffing, when he's got the winning hand—and WHY. Based on accurate investigation; it is NOT guesswork. Even the greatest of gamblers has some giveaway behavior. For the first time in print, one of the world's top poker players reveals how he virtually can read minds because nearly every player has a "tell." Seal the leaks in your poker game and empty your opponent's chip tray.
Hardbound. $20.00. (ISBN: 0-914314-04-1)

The Gambling Times Official Rules of Poker by Mike Caro—Settles home poker arguments. Caro has written the revised rule book (including a section on etiquette) for the Horseshoe Club in Gardena, California, that may soon be adopted by other clubs and become the California standard. He is presently scheduling a meeting of poker room managers

at the Bingo Palace in Las Vegas. This should lead to the creation of a uniform book of rules for Nevada cardrooms. *The Gambling Times Official Rules of Poker* includes sections of the rules from public cardrooms, but mostly it is for home poker. The book is needed because there presently exists no true authority for settling Friday night poker disputes.
Softbound. $5.95. (ISBN: 0-89746-012-X)

Poker for Women by Mike Caro—How women can take advantage of the special male-female ego wars at the poker table and win. This book also has non-poker everyday value for women. Men can be destroyed at the poker table by coy, cunning or aggressive women. That's because, on a subconscious level, men expect women to act traditionally. This book tells women when to flirt, when to be tough and when to whimper. Many of the tactics are tried and proven by Caro's own students. This book does not claim that women are better players, merely that there are strategies available to them that are not available to their male opponents.
Softbound. $5.95. (ISBN: 0-89746-009-X)

Poker Without Cards by Mike Caro—Applying world-class poker tactics to everyday life. Is the salesman bluffing? Can you get a better price? Negotiating is like playing a poker hand. Although poker tactics are common in daily encounters, few people realize when a hand is being played. It's hard to make the right decision when you're not even aware that you've been raised. The book is honest and accurate in its evaluation of behavior.
Softbound. $6.95. (ISBN: 0-89746-038-3)

Win, Places, and Pros by Tex Sheahan—With more than 50 years of experience as a professional poker player and cardroom manager/tournament director, Tex lets his readers in on the secrets that separate the men from the boys at the poker table. Descriptions of poker events, playing experiences from all over the world, and those special personalities who are the masters of the game. . .Tex knows them all and lays it out in his marvelous easy-to-read style.
Softbound. $6.95. (ISBN: 0-89746-008-1)

Blackjack Books

The Beginner's Guide to Winning Blackjack by Stanley Roberts—The world's leading blackjack writer shows beginners to the game how to obtain an instant advantage through the simplest of techniques. Covering Basic Strategy for all major casino areas from Las Vegas to the Bahamas, Atlantic City and Reno/Tahoe, Roberts provides a simple system to immediately know when the remaining cards favor the player. The entire method can be learned in less than two hours and taken to the casinos to produce sure profits.
Softbound. $10.00. (ISBN: 0-89746-014-6)

The Gambling Times Guide to Blackjack by Stanley Roberts with Edward O. Thorp, Ken Uston, Lance Humble, Arnold Snyder, Julian Braun, Richard Canfield and other experts in this field—The top blackjack authorities have been brought together for the first time to bring to the reader the ins and outs of the game of blackjack. All aspects of the game are discussed. Winning techniques are presented for beginners and casual players.
Softbound. $5.95. (ISBN: 0-89746-015-4)

Million Dollar Blackjack by Ken Uston—Every blackjack enthusiast or gaming traveler who fancies himself a "21" player can improve his game with this explosive bestseller. Ken Uston shows you how he and his team won over 4 million dollars at blackjack. Now, for the first time, you can find out how he did it and how his system can help you. Includes playing and betting strategies, winning secrets, protection from cheaters, Uston's Advanced Point Count System, and a glossary of inside terms used by professionals. More than 50,000 copies in print.
Hardbound. $18.95. (ISBN: 0-914314-08-4)

Casino Games

The Gambling Times Guide to Casino Games by Len Miller—The co-founder and editor of *Gambling Times* magazine vividly describes the casino games and explains their rules and betting procedures. This easy-to-follow guide covers blackjack, craps, roulette, keno, video machines, progressive slots and more. After reading this book, you'll play like a pro!
Softbound. $5.95. (ISBN: 0-89746-017-0)

The Gambling Times Guide to Craps by N.B. Winkless, Jr.—The ultimate craps book for beginners and experts alike. It provides you with a program to tackle the house edge that can be used on a home computer. This text shows you which bets to avoid and tells you the difference between craps in Nevada and craps in other gaming resort areas. It includes a glossary of terms and a directory of dealer schools. Softbound. $5.95. (ISBN: 0-89746-013-8)

General Interest Books

According to Gambling Times: The Rules of Gambling Games by Stanley Roberts—At last you can finally settle all the arguments regarding what the rules are in every known gambling endeavor. From pari-mutuels to bookie slips, from blackjack to gin rummy, the rules of the games and the variations that are generally accepted in both public and private situations are clearly enumerated by the world's #1 gaming authority. Hardbound. $12.00. (ISBN: 0-914314-07-6)

The Gambling Times Guide to Gaming Around the World compiled by Arnold L. Abrams—The complete travel guide to legal gaming throughout the world. This comprehensive gaming guide lists casinos around the world; the games played in each; cardrooms and facilities; greyhound racing and horse racing tracks, as well as jai alai frontons, lotteries and sports betting facilities. This book is a must for the traveling gamer. Softbound. $5.95. (ISBN: 0-89746-020-0)

The Gambling Times Guide to Systems That Win, Volume I and Volume II—For those who want to broaden their gambling knowledge, this two-volume set offers complete gambling systems used by the experts. Learn their strategies and how to incorporate them into your gambling style. **Volume I** covers 12 systems that win for roulette, craps, backgammon, slot machines, horse racing, baseball, basketball and football. Softbound. $5.95. (ISBN: 0-89746-034-0) **Volume II** features 12 more systems that win, covering horse racing, craps, blackjack, slot machines, jai alai and baseball. Softbound. $5.95. (ISBN: 0-89746-034-0)

The Gambling Times Guide to Winning Systems, Volume I and Volume II—For those who take their gambling seriously, *Gambling Times* presents a two-volume set of proven winning systems. Learn how the experts beat the house edge and become consistent winners. **Volume I** contains 12 complete strategies for casino games and sports wagering, including baccarat, blackjack, keno, basketball and harness handicapping.
Softbound. $5.95. (ISBN: 0-89746-032-4)
Volume II contains 12 more winning systems covering poker bluffing, pitching analysis, greyhound handicapping and roulette.
Softbound. $5.95. (ISBN: 0-89746-033-2)

Gambling Times Presents Winning Systems and Methods, Volume I and Volume II—This two-volume collection of winning strategies by some of the nation's leading experts on gambling will help you in your quest to beat the percentages. **Volume I** includes several chapters on blackjack, as well as methods for beating baseball, basketball, hockey, steeplechase and grass racing.
Softbound. $5.95. (ISBN: 0-89746-036-7)
Volume II contains an analysis of keno and video poker, as well as systems for success in sports betting and horse racing.
Softbound. $5.95. (ISBN: 0-89746-037-5)

The Mathematics of Gambling by Edward O. Thorp—The "Albert Einstein of gambling" presents his second book on the subject. His first book, *Beat The Dealer,* set the gambling world on its heels and struck fear into the cold-blooded hearts of Las Vegas casino-owners in 1962. Now, more than twenty years later, Dr. Thorp again challenges the odds by bringing out a simple to understand version of more than thirty years of exploration into all aspects of what separates winners from losers. . . knowing the real meaning of the parameters of the games.
Softbound. $7.95. (ISBN: 0-89746-019-7)

Odds: Quick and Simple by Mike Caro—How to know the right lines and win by figuring the odds logically. Common sense replaces mathematical formulas. This book will teach probabilities plainly and powerfully. The emphasis will be on gambling, showing how to quickly determine whether or not to make a wager. Particular emphasis will be on sports bets, pot odds in poker, dice and various proposition bets. Also

included will be tables of the most important gambling odds (craps, roulette, poker, blackjack, keno) for easy reference.
Softbound. $5.95. (ISBN: 0-89746-030-8)

P$yching Out Vegas by Marvin Karlins, Ph.D.—The dream merchants who build and operate gaming resorts subtly work on the casino patron to direct his attention, control his actions and turn his pockets inside out. At last, their techniques are revealed to you by a noted psychologist who shows you how you can successfully control your behavior and turn a losing attitude into a lifetime winning streak.
Hardbound. $12.00. (ISBN: 0-914314-03-3)

Winning by Computer by Dr. Donald Sullivan—Now, for the first time, the wonders of computer technology are harnessed for the gambler. Dr. Sullivan explains how to figure the odds and identify key factors in all forms of race and sports handicapping.
Softbound. $5.95. (ISBN: 0-89746-018-9)

Sports Betting Books

The Gambling Times Guide to Basketball Handicapping by Barbara Nathan—This easy-to-read, highly informative book is the definitive guide to basketball betting. Expert sports handicapper Barbara Nathan provides handicapping knowledge, insightful coverage, and step-by-step guidance for money management. The advantages and disadvantages of relying on sports services are also covered.
Softbound. $5.95. (ISBN: 0-89746-023-5)

The Gambling Times Guide to Football Handicapping by Bob McCune— Starting with the novice's approach to handicapping football, and winding up with some of the more sophisticated team selection techniques in the sports handicapping realm, this book will actually tell the reader how to forecast, *in advance,* the final scores of most major national football games. The author's background and expertise on the subject will put money into any sports gambler's pocket.
Softbound. $5.95. (ISBN: 0-89746-022-7)

The Gambling Times Guide to Greyhound Racing by William E. McBride—This complete discussion of greyhound racing is a must for anyone who is just beginning to appreciate this exciting and profitable sport. The book begins with a brief overview detailing the origins of greyhound racing and pari-mutuel betting, and explains the greyhound track environment, betting procedures, and handicapping methods. Includes an appendix of various greyhound organizations, a review of greyhound books, and an interesting section on famous dogs and personalities in the world of greyhound racing.
Softbound. $5.95. (ISBN: 0-89746-007-3)

The Gambling Times Guide to Jai Alai by William R. Keevers—The most comprehensive book on jai alai available. Author Bill Keevers takes the reader on an informative journey from the ancient beginnings of the game to its current popularity. This easy-to-understand guide will show you the fine points of the game, how to improve your betting percentage, and where to find jai alai frontons.
Softbound. $5.95. (ISBN: 0-89746-010-3)

The Gambling Times Guide to Thoroughbred Racing by R.G. Denis—Newcomers to the racetrack and veterans alike will appreciate the informative description of the thoroughbred pari-mutuel activity supplied by this experienced racing authority. Activities at the track and available information are blended skillfully in this guide to selecting winners that pay off in big-ticket returns.
Softbound. $5.95. (ISBN: 0-89746-005-7)

UPCOMING *GAMBLING TIMES* BOOKS

The following books will be at your local bookstore by September, 1984. If you can't find them there, they may also be ordered directly from *Gambling Times*.

Poker Books

Caro's Poker Encyclopedia by Mike Caro—Features alphabetical definitions and discussions of poker terms. Extensively cross-indexed, it can be used as a reference book to look up important poker terms (ante, bluff, sandbag) or it can be pleasurably read straight through. The definitions are brief; the advice is in-depth.
Softbound. $8.95. (ISBN: 0-89746-039-1)

Free Money: How to Win in the Cardrooms of California by Michael Wiesenberg—Computer expert and poker writer par excellence, Michael Wiesenberg delivers critical knowledge to those who play in the poker rooms of the western states. Wiesenberg gives you the precise meaning of the rules as well as the mathematics of poker to aid public and private poker players alike. Wiesenberg, a prolific author, is published by more gaming periodicals than any other writer.
Softbound. $6.95. (ISBN: 0-89746-027-8)

New Poker Games by Mike Caro—Features descriptions and winning strategies for well-thought-out but never-before-introduced forms of poker. Caro has already created two games: Caro Dots (through *Gambling Times*) and Tic Tac Hold 'Em. Tic Tac Hold 'Em was launched via a tournament held at the Imperial Palace in Las Vegas. While anyone can devise a new form of poker, few games are logically balanced. If a game isn't fine-tuned, illogical sequences of betting may occur, making the game strategically weak. Here is a collection of brand new games to liven up your next Friday night sessions.
Softbound. $5.95. (ISBN: 0-89746-040-5)

PROfile: The World's Greatest Poker Players by Stuart Jacobs—From background information, to style of play and ratings, this book adds personal interviews with all the poker greats, from the Grand Old Man of Poker, Johnny Moss, to the top women players like Betty Carey. If you

want to play like them, you'll need to read this book. If you want to play against them, you'd better read this book...first.
Hardbound. $15.00. (ISBN: 0-914314-05-X)

The Railbird by Rex Jones—The ultimate kibitzer, the man who watches from the rail in the poker room, has unique insights into the character and performance of all poker players. From this vantage point, Rex Jones, Ph.D., blends his expertise and considerable education in anthropology with his lifetime of poker playing and watching. The result is a delightful book with exceptional values for those who want to avoid the fatal errors of bad players and capitalize upon the qualities that make up the winning strengths of outstanding poker players.
Softbound. $6.95. (ISBN: 0-89746-028-6)

Tales Out of Tulsa by Bobby Baldwin—Oklahoma-born Bobby Baldwin, the youngest player to ever win the World Championship of Poker, is considered to be among the top five poker players in the world. Known affectionately as "The Owl," this brilliant poker genius, wise beyond his years, brings the benefits of his experience to the pages of this book. It's sure to stop the leaks in your poker game, and you will be amazingly ahead of your opponents in the very next game you play.
Softbound. $6.95. (ISBN: 0-89746-006-5)

World Class Poker, Play by Play by Mike Caro—Once again, Caro brings the world of poker to life. This time he gives us a one-card-at-a-time analysis of world class poker, with many card illustrations. This book includes discussions of professional tactics, then simulates game situations and asks the reader to make decisions. Next, Caro provides the answer and the hand continues. This learn-while-you-pretend-to-play format is a favorite teaching method of Caro's and one which meets with a great deal of success.
Hardbound. $20.00. (ISBN: 0-914314-06-08)

General Interest Books

Caro on Computer Gambling by Mike Caro—Caro discusses computers and how they will change gambling. He provides winning systems and descriptions of actual programs. This book will give the novice a taste of how computers work. Using the Pascal programming language, Caro

builds a working program step-by-step to show how a computer thinks and, also, how a human should analyze gambling propositions. This book is only slightly technical and mostly logical. Also discussed are ways that computers can cheat and speculation on the future of computers in gambling. Will you be able to type in your horse bets from your home computer? Can that personal computer be linked by phone into a perpetual poker game with the pots going straight into your bank account? The answers to these questions are found right here in Caro's book.
Softbound. $6.95. (ISBN: 0-89746-042-1)

The Casinos of the Caribbean by Stanley Roberts—The ultimate coffee-table book, in full color, showing the exotic vacation resorts of the Caribbean. Emphasis is placed on the casino activity on each island, with travel information, gaming advice and important shopping tips. As lush as the region it depicts, this volume will be the envy of your guests. Hardbound. $25.00. (ISBN: 0-914314-09-2)

The Casino Gourmet: Great Recipes from the Master Chefs of... by Stanley Roberts—This unique six-volume set showcases the top hotel restaurants in the resort areas of Las Vegas, Atlantic City, Reno/Lake Tahoe, the Caribbean, Europe and the Orient. For each restaurant, complete meals are featured, with recipes for the entrees and "Chef's Suggestions" for every appropriate item from appetizer to dessert. Comparable to classic coffee-table art books, each volume features color photographs of the hotels, casinos and restaurants.

The Casino Gourmet: Great Recipes from the Master Chefs of Las Vegas. Hardbound. $20.00. (ISBN: 0-914314-10-6)

The Casino Gourmet: Great Recipes from the Master Chefs of Atlantic City. Hardbound. $20.00. (ISBN: 0-914314-11-4)

The Casino Gourmet: Great Recipes from the Master Chefs of Reno/Lake Tahoe. Hardbound. $20.00. (ISBN: 0-914314-12-2)

The Casino Gourmet: Great Recipes from the Master Chefs of the Caribbean. Hardbound. $20.00. (ISBN: 0-914314-13-0)

The Casino Gourmet: Great Recipes from the Master Chefs of Europe. Hardbound. $20.00. (ISBN: 0-914314-14-9)

The Casino Gourmet: Great Recipes from the Master Chefs of the Orient. Hardbound. $20.00. (ISBN: 0-914314-15-7)

A Gambler's View of History by Mike Caro—Who was drawn out on, who made bad bets but then got lucky, and who was bluffed out in world affairs. Fun reading. Along the way, the reader may get some insights into how gambling tactics affect everyday, real-life decisions. It's Caro's contention that any world leader who truly understands probability has a much better chance of success. Unfortunately, leaders find themselves faced with once-in-a-lifetime situations. In these, they can easily make the correct decision and still meet disaster. Caro calls that "the equivalent of raising with a full house before the draw, but being unable to prevent an opponent from making a straight flush." Sometimes historic figures looked good even though they made wrong decisions; sometimes these historic figures made all the right decisions but did not look good. In this book, Caro explores the "whys and wherefores" of this seeming paradox.
Softbound. $7.95. (ISBN: 0-89746-043-X)

Gambling Greats: Profiles of the World's Greatest Gamblers by Pamela Shandel—From the legendary "Titanic" Thompson and Nick "The Greek" Dandelos, to the current heroes of the gambling scene such as Ed Thorp, Ken Uston and Stanley Roberts at blackjack; Johnny Moss, Doyle Brunson, Stu Ungar at poker; and a host of top backgammon, gin rummy and other gambling superstars, author Pamela Shandel details the lives, skills and significant events that make up the lore of gambling.
Hardbound. $14.00. (ISBN: 0-914314-16-5)

The Gambling Times Quiz Book by Mike Caro—Learn while testing your knowledge. Caro's book includes questions and answers on the concepts and information published in previous issues of *Gambling Times*. Caro tells why an answer is correct and credit is given to the author whose *Gambling Times* article suggested the question. This book covers only established fact, not the personal opinions of authors, and Caro's inimitable style makes this an easy-reading, easy-learning book.
Softbound. $5.95. (ISBN: 0-89746-031-6)

How the Superstars Gamble by Ron Delpit—Follow the stars to the racetracks, ball games, casinos and private clubs. You'll be amazed at how involved these world famous personalities are in the gambling scene, and how clever they are at the games they play. Ron Delpit, lifelong horse racing fan and confidant of innumerable showbiz greats, tells you fascinating tales about his friends, the superstars, with startling heretofore secret facts.
Hardbound. $12.00. (ISBN: 0-914314-17-3)

How to Win at Gaming Tournaments by Haven Earle Haley—Win your share of the millions of dollars and fabulous prizes being awarded to gaming contestants, and have the glory of being a World Champion. Poker, gin rummy, backgammon, craps, blackjack and baccarat are all popular tournament games. The rules, special tournament regulations, playing procedures, and how to obtain free entry are fully explained in this informative manual. The tournament promoters—who they are, where they hold events—and the cash and prizes awarded are explained in detail. Tournament play usually requires special strategy changes, which are detailed in this book.
Softbound. $8.95. (ISBN: 0-89746-016-2)

You're Comped: How to Be a Casino Guest by Len Miller—If you're a player you don't have to pay! Learn how to be "comped" in luxury casino-resort hotels the world over. A list of casinos together with names and addresses of junket representatives are included in this revealing guidebook. How to handle yourself on a junket is important if you want to receive all that you've been promised and be invited back again. How to do this, along with what you can expect from the casino, is explained in detail.
Softbound. $7.95. (ISBN: 0-89746-041-3)

Sports Betting Books

Cramer on Harness Race Handicapping by Mark Cramer—This systematic analysis of nuances in past performances will uncover patterns of improvement which will lead to flat bet profits. This book provides a functioning balance between creative handicapping and mechanical application.
Softbound. $6.95. (ISBN: 0-89746-026-X)

Cramer on Thoroughbred Handicapping by Mark Cramer—A unique approach to selecting winners, with price in mind, by distinguishing between valuable and common-place information. Results: higher average pay-offs and solid flat bet profits. How to spot signs of improvement and when to cash in. And much, much more. Softbound. $6.95. (ISBN: 0-89746-025-1)

Ordering Information

Send your book order along with your check or money order to:

Gambling Times
1018 N. Cole Ave.
Hollywood, CA 90038

Softbound Books: Please add $1.00 per book if delivered in the United States, $1.50 in Canada or Mexico, and $3.50 for foreign countries.

Hardbound Books: Shipping charges for the following books are $2.50 if delivered in the United States, $3.00 in Canada or Mexico, and $5.00 for foreign countries:

According to Gambling Times: The Rules of Gambling Games
Caro's Book of Tells
The Casino Gourmet: Great Recipes from the Master Chefs of Atlantic City
The Casino Gourmet: Great Recipes from the Master Chefs of the Carribean
The Casino Gourmet: Great Recipes from the Master Chefs of Europe
The Casino Gourmet: Great Recipes from the Master Chefs of Las Vegas
The Casino Gourmet: Great Recipes from the Master Chefs of the Orient
The Casino Gourmet: Great Recipes from the Master Chefs of Reno/ Lake Tahoe
The Casinos of the Carribean
Gambling Greats: Profiles of the World's Greatest Gamblers
How the Superstars Gamble
Million Dollar Blackjack
PROfile: The World's Greatest Poker Players
P$yching Out Vegas
World Class Poker, Play by Play